TV & MOVIE FACTS

The photographs in this book are courtesy of the following organizations:
Movie Star News; Museum of Modern Art/Film Stills Archive; Warner Bros.; Columbia Pictures Home Video; Universal City Studios; United Artists; Columbia Pictures Industries, Inc.; 20th Century-Fox Television.

Researched and written by: Walter J. Podrazik.
Cover design: Jeff Hapner.

ISBN 0-88176-321-7

PRINTED IN CANADA

Introduction

Any time you go to a movie or watch a show on TV you hope to be entertained and involved, to be moved to laughter or tears, to be made to think, to find excitement or adventure. And that's just when you watch what's on the screen. What you *see*, though, is only half the story: What went on behind the scenes is often even more fascinating, and this book lets you in on some of those backstage details.

Find out here, for instance, which movie introduced Humphrey Bogart to Lauren Bacall and sparked their real-life romance. Find out whose initials were on James Bond's silver Aston Martin in *Goldfinger;* who was bumped from the lead role in the 1985 summer hit *Back to the Future* in favor of Michael J. Fox; and what "anhedonia" means (it was a suggested title for Woody Allen's *Annie Hall*).

These and hundreds of other intriguing and unusual bits of information make up the movie section of this book; and there's lots more of the same in the TV section. Do you know what the acronym TARDIS (Doctor Who's space-travel vehicle) stands for? Can you name the pilot show for *Happy Days?* Do you know why several different endings were filmed for the famous *Dallas* episode where it was finally revealed who shot J.R.?

Find all the answers here, in this handy, take-with treasure chest of facts, figures, anecdotes, and information about favorite movies and TV shows.

FACTS ABOUT THE MOVIES

Sci-Fi & Fantasy

BACK TO THE FUTURE (1985)

Robert Zemeckis had been pitching *Back to the Future* for several years. Then, following his success with *Romancing the Stone*, everything started falling into place.

Perhaps the most difficult moment in the project came when Zemeckis decided that the lead he had chosen (Eric Stolz, star of *Mask*) was not quite right for the lighter comedy-romance style of *Back to the Future.* Though he was already $4 million and five weeks into shooting, he replaced Stolz with Michael J. Fox (co-star of TV's *Family Ties*).

Fox stepped into a very strange shooting schedule. He had to film *Back to the Future* during the evenings after working on the *Family Ties* series during the days.

Nonetheless, Fox's characterization meshed perfectly with the script and *Back to the Future* became one of the biggest box-office smashes of the summer of '85.

BLADE RUNNER (1982)

To build a believable version of Los Angeles in 2019, the makers of *Blade Runner* took over the old Warner Bros.' "New York" street set where literally hundreds of movies had been shot (from *The Maltese Falcon* and *The Big Sleep* to *Hello Dolly!* and *Annie*) and turned it into the punk/*film noir*/art deco urban nightmare that the film crew nicknamed Ridleyville after director Ridley Scott. To do this, the set was "retrofitted" with air-conditioning ducts, electrical cables, heavy machinery, and $100,000 worth of neon signs, which was all the budget would allow plus all that could be salvaged from the 1982 film *One From the Heart*.

Noted industrial designer Syd Mead, who had helped build the Concorde, invented a unique hydraulic steering system for the flying, "spinner" cars he created for *Blade Runner*. He also contributed other futuristic vehicles, weapons, telephones, and parking meters.

For the model cityscape used for aerial views of Ridleyville in *Blade Runner*, the Entertainment Effects Group borrowed miniature skyscrapers left over from *Escape From New York*. They even took a model of the *Star Wars* spaceship *Millennium Falcon*, and balanced it on end to make an instant skyscraper.

CLOSE ENCOUNTERS OF THE THIRD KIND (1977)

For *Close Encounters of the Third Kind*, Steven Spielberg went back to an old idea entitled *Night Skies*, which was a story about an average American meeting creatures from outer space. Having made a home movie at the age of 16 called *Firefight*, about hostile aliens, Spielberg now wanted to do one about benign aliens.

According to UFOlogist Allen Hynek, close encounters of the third kind are those involving actual contact with extra-terrestrials. Close encounters of the first kind are simple UFO sightings; those of the second kind are sightings that leave behind physical evidence.

For *Close Encounters*, Spielberg could not locate a soundstage large enough to accommodate the film's climax and was forced to shoot in an abandoned dirigible hangar in Mobile, Alabama.

For Carlo Rimbaldi, who created the alien for *Close Encounters*, it was the first of a number of such assignments: He created other extraterrestrials for Ridley Scott's *Alien* (1979) and Spielberg's *E.T.—The Extra-Terrestrial* (1982).

The alien children in *Close Encounters* were real children in rubber suits. At first Spielberg put them on roller skates so they would glide rather than walk, but the ruse was not a success—the children kept falling over.

Special effects expert Douglas Trumbull gave the Mothership its unique "chandelier" look by studding the surface with tiny light bulbs and bits from model kits—including kits for a Volkswagen, a mailbox, a toy shark, and a model of R2-D2.

Two versions of *Close Encounters of the Third Kind* are available to viewers. The second, in which Richard Dreyfuss actually enters the

Close Encounters of the Third Kind

Mothership, is the film Spielberg claims he wanted to make all along.

E.T.—THE EXTRA-TERRESTRIAL (1982)

The character of E.T. was kept a well-guarded secret on the set of Steven Spielberg's *E.T.—The Extra-Terrestrial.* No visitors were allowed on the set and no stills were released. Spielberg didn't even let the publicity department see E.T., so the publicists were faced with the problem of designing a poster for a film they knew nothing about. They came up with a poster which showed a misshapen finger wrapping itself around the edge of a door.

Designer Carlo Rimbaldi made several E.T.s for different activities. Depending on the scene, E.T. moved through the use of radio-controlled devices, hand puppets, or midgets in E.T. suits.

Because Rimbaldi was facing an immovable deadline, he enlisted the help of Craig Reardon to finish E.T. Reardon was responsible for painting E.T. and creating the extra-terrestrial's eyes.

The glowing heart of E.T. caused a lot of difficulty. E.T. was made of heavy latex and anything bright enough to show through it would also be hot enough to set the little extra-terrestrial on fire. So a separate E.T. chest was fabricated out of transparent plastic. Inside were several organs, which moved when air was pumped into them, and a bright light. The chest was then painted with translucent paint, and on command the chest lit up and the organs moved. A separate suit with a light was designed for the midget.

To achieve the desired alien effect for E.T.'s voice, 18 different animals were recorded and the sounds synthesized. The animals included raccoons, cats, and horses. When E.T. learned to speak English, distorted human voices were used. Actress Debra Winger read much of his dialogue.

Elliott's use of Reese's® Pieces (made by the Hershey Foods Corp.) to lure E.T. out of hiding was not a matter of chance. The company paid to have their product featured. M&M/Mars were the first to be approached about having M&Ms® featured, but they balked at the modest price they'd have to pay for this exposure.

RAIDERS OF THE LOST ARK (1981)

When United Artists released *Raiders of the Lost Ark* and the James Bond film *For Your Eyes Only* in June of 1981, *Raiders* beat Bond three to one at the box office. Steven Spielberg had made a better Bond.

Rather than spend another day in the 130-degree heat of the Tunisia location, Harrison

Ford suggested speeding up the whip vs. scimitar scene in the marketplace where Indiana Jones rescues Marion (Karen Allen). Why not, he said, have Indy pull out a gun and shoot the Turk? Then they could all go home. It turned out to be one of the favorite scenes in the movie.

Philip Kaufman (*The Right Stuff*) was the person who came up with the plotline to *Raiders of the Lost Ark*—the search for the lost Ark of the Covenant. His orthodontist had told him about the Ark when Kaufman was nine.

STAR TREK—THE MOTION PICTURE (1979)

Over the years, rumors had abounded among the fanatic fans (who call themselves "Trekkers") of the TV series *Star Trek* that some/most/all of the cast would return: in a one-shot TV movie, in a limited run TV series, or (best of all) in a wide-screen feature film. Their incessant interest helped spur Paramount Pictures into approaching the program's creator, Gene Roddenberry, and the original cast about a reunion.

In Roddenberry's first script for the film, the crew of the starship *Enterprise* came across a creature claiming to be God. Paramount balked at that scenario, but eventually an acceptable script was hammered out—featuring an all-powerful creature that was causing a disturbance in space.

The key cast member for the film was Leonard Nimoy, who played Mr. Spock, the series' most popular character. At first Nimoy did not want to make the film, claiming he already had enough trouble trying to disassociate himself from the character. Eventually, the deal offered proved too sweet to resist. By the third feature film, though, it took an offer to direct the picture to lure him in.

Star Trek had a budget of about $40 million. This allowed for more elaborate settings, effects, and costuming than on the TV series. For instance, the entire spaceship *Enterprise* had never been shown on TV, so the model had been painted on one side only. In the movie, the camera slowly circled the entire ship, as it waited in dock, to show every detail.

The costume budget included 12 yards of material (red, black, silver, and gold brocade) that had been purchased by Cecil B. DeMille in 1938—and was valued at $20,000. This was used for the costume worn by the ambassador from Betelgeuse, making it one of the most expensive costumes ever.

Despite this attention to detail, the film itself seemed to lack the heart of the series, leaving all but the truly dedicated disappointed. Paramount was also disappointed. Though the film did okay at the box office, the studio made it clear that any future films would have to be made on a much tighter budget.

STAR TREK II: THE WRATH OF KHAN (1982)

Before beginning work on the second *Star Trek* movie, director Nicholas Meyer sat down and watched every episode of the television series. This gave him a much better feel for what made the program and the characters work. As a result, *Star Trek II* was superior to the first theatrical film, with a better story, better pacing, and an effective sense of humor.

Subtitled *The Wrath of Khan*, the film was a follow-up to a 1967 episode from the original TV series called "Space Seed," picking up the story some 15 years later. Ricardo Montalban repeated his television role as the villainous Khan, and won rave reviews.

At the end, Mr. Spock died—though no one in the theater (or at Paramount) really believed that this was true.

STAR TREK III: THE SEARCH FOR SPOCK (1984)

When asked what it would take to lure him back for another *Star Trek* film, Leonard Nimoy said he'd like to direct it. Much to his surprise, the studio agreed.

The key questions of the film were: Was Spock really alive? Where was he? And would Kirk find him—in time? During publicity for the movie, William Shatner noted that the answers were fairly obvious. After all, they couldn't come to the end of a movie subtitled *The Search for Spock* and turn to the audience and say: "Sorry, we looked but we couldn't find him!"

STAR WARS (1977)

The saga that started a production empire began in a relatively small way. Sound man Ben Burtt created most of the initial movie's sound effects in director George Lucas' basement, using a tape recorder and his collection of artillery and explosion sounds. (The engine noise for the *Mil-*

lennium Falcon spaceship came from a P-51 World War II Mustang.)

Once *Star Wars* hit big, profits were used not only for a sequel but also to establish special effects production facilities (Industrial Light and Magic) that could be used by other filmmakers.

Star Wars was originally presented as a self-contained saga that left room for a sequel (the villainous Darth Vader escaped at the end). However, when the follow-up, *The Empire Strikes Back*, opened in 1980, audiences were amazed to see the screen titles identify that film as "Episode V" of the *Star Wars* saga.

George Lucas then revealed that the two films (and a third one already in the works) were the center trilogy of a projected nine-film series. Upon re-release, the first *Star Wars* movie carried slightly revised opening titles which identified it as "Episode IV: A New Hope."

In 1983, *Return of the Jedi* ("Episode VI") completed the middle trilogy. However, Lucas gave no indication as to when (if ever) the remaining films would be made.

SUPERMAN (1978)

Before Christopher Reeve got the film role of *Superman*, which flew him to stardom, the role had been turned down by Robert Redford and Paul Newman. Newman also turned down the part of Lex Luthor, which subsequently went to Gene Hackman. Many were considered for the role of Superman, including producer Ilya Salkind's wife's dentist.

Superman II

In order to become Superman, Christopher Reeve, skinny at the time he was chosen for the role, had to go through a muscle and weight building regimen. It worked; he didn't have to pad his Superman suit.

Carrie Fisher, who had just completed *Star Wars*, was suggested for the role of Lois Lane. However, when Margot Kidder was brought to London from her home in Montana for a test, Superman had his Lois.

It took 350 days and 1,250,000 feet of film to complete *Superman*, but in an innovative move the producers simultaneously filmed scenes for *Superman* and *Superman II*, which was released in 1980.

One of the largest soundstages in the world—often used for the James Bond films—became Superman's icy Fortress of Solitude. To create the effect of ice, $6000 of salt was scattered. The submarine from the 1977 Bond movie *The Spy Who Loved Me* was rigged to support several ice floes.

*M*arlon Brando signed to play Jor-El, Superman's father, for the hefty figure of $4 million. The *Superman* crew calculated Brando's salary to be $8 per second. They figured that if Brando were to buy a Rolls Royce, by the time it reached Shepperton Studios it would be paid for. Gene Hackman came on board for $2 million.

Horror & Monster Movies

THE EXORCIST (1973)

*M*akeup whiz Dick Smith used a specially made, life-size dummy to achieve one of the most horrific scenes in moviemaking—the scene in *The Exorcist* where young Linda Blair's head appears to rotate 360 degrees.

*M*ost of the heavy-duty special effects for *The Exorcist* were done on a refrigerated set so that the actors' breath would be visible. These scenes were shot in temperatures between 0°F and 10°F, much to the discomfort of the cast and crew.

*I*n the book of *The Exorcist*, the priest played on the screen by Max Von Sydow performs the exorcism, but in the movie his character dies before the exorcism takes place and the ritual is actually performed by the priest assisting him, played by Jason Miller. The reason for the change? Von Sydow is an atheist, and he couldn't bring the necessary conviction to the priest's lines he was required to speak.

FRANKENSTEIN (1931)

The embodiment of Frankenstein's monster in the 1931 screen classic was the work of Jack Pierce. He painstakingly built up actor Boris Karloff's forehead to make it look as though Frankenstein had simply sawed off the top of the creature's head in order to insert the brain; then Pierce increased the monster's bulk with padding and his height with the thick-soled, weighted boots that also caused his stiff, forward-leaning walk.

The transformation of man into monster for *Frankenstein* took four hours, plus another four hours to reverse the process. This time-consuming makeup routine, combined with Universal's desire to keep the monster's appearance secret until the premiere, meant that Boris Karloff got very little opportunity to socialize with anyone else on the set of the movie.

One of *Frankenstein's* most infamous scenes, in which the monster throws a little girl into the stream, expecting her to float like a flower, was cut after the premiere. The child drowns instead of floating, and the scene so upset the premiere audience that it was removed—with the approval of director James Whale, who wasn't satisfied with the scene anyway.

In 1936, weary of being tagged as a horror film director, James Whale made a film totally out of character with *Frankenstein* and his other horror standards—the Jerome Kern musical *Showboat.*

HALLOWEEN (1978)

*H*alloween, made in just three weeks and on a budget of $320,000, grossed more than 50 million dollars, thus becoming one of the most profitable independent movies ever made.

Halloween supposedly takes place on Halloween night in Haddonfield, Illinois. In fact, it was shot in May in a suburb of Los Angeles. Bushels of dead leaves were scattered on the lawns to create an autumnal effect—but the viewer who looks closely will see that the trees are still green. Even the pumpkins had to be faked: The art director sent to South America for pumpkin-shaped gourds and then had them painted orange.

John Carpenter, director of *Halloween* and a dedicated movie buff, makes playful allusions to favorite movies in his films. In *Halloween,* for instance, the psychiatrist is named Sam Loomis, the name of the John Gavin character in *Psycho*; and the sheriff is named Lee Brackett after screenwriter Leigh Brackett, who worked on *The Big Sleep* and *Rio Bravo.* Similarly in *Escape From New York* minor characters are named after fellow horror film directors George Romero and David Cronenberg.

JAWS (1975)

Peter Benchley, author of *Jaws,* is the son of screenwriter Nathaniel Benchley (*The Russians Are Coming, The Russians Are Coming*) and grandson of humorist Robert Benchley.

Author Benchley had a small part in *Jaws* as a TV reporter.

Several directors were interviewed about doing *Jaws.* One lost the job because he kept referring to the shark as a whale. Steven Spielberg finally got the assignment.

Producers David Brown and Richard Zanuck were confident that for *Jaws* they could find a great white shark that was trainable. They soon discovered that dolphins are trainable, sharks are not.

If you can't find a big shark, use a small stuntman. Former jockey Carl Rizzo doubled for Richard Dreyfuss in the scenes where Dreyfuss' character, Matt Hooper, goes underwater. Rizzo is seen in a shark cage 5/8 of the normal cage size, which made the shark look enormous.

The model shark used in *Jaws* was affectionately named Bruce—after Steven Speilberg's attorney.

Bob Mattey, who created Flash Gordon's rockets and the giant squid in *20,000 Leagues Under the Sea,* came out of retirement to make the model shark. In fact, three 25-foot models were made—one with the jaws closed, and two with them open.

The Coast Guard crew that worked on the film was of such great assistance that Universal asked what the studio could do in return. The answer: Design new uniforms for its female members. It may be the only Coast Guard contingent in which the women wear Edith Head originals.

KING KONG (1933)

King Kong was the brainchild of Merian C. Cooper, journalist, explorer, and former pilot.

Willis O'Brien was taken off an RKO film called *Creation* (which was then abandoned) to work on creating a believable giant ape for *King Kong*. Some of the footage from *Creation* can be spotted in *King Kong* and *Son of Kong*.

Long shots of the ape in *King Kong* were miniatures, but it was necessary to create a life-size bust of Kong's head and hand. It took 40 bearskins to cover the bust.

Actress Fay Wray had to spend hours standing in Kong's mechanical hand ten feet above the ground during the filming. She had to kick, scream, and squirm around in the huge hand, and in doing so loosened the great ape's mechanical grip. Every so often the hand would open completely and Wray would be left dangling, hanging on to Kong's thumb for dear life.

King Kong's roar was created by taking a tape of a lion's roar, running it backwards, and re-recording it. The high spots and the loud peaks were spliced together, and re-recorded to produce a roar majestic enough for Kong.

NIGHT OF THE LIVING DEAD (1968)

Night of the Living Dead was shot in—of all places—Pittsburgh. George Romero, the movie's director, co-writer, cinematographer, and editor, has lived and worked in Pittsburgh for most of his career. The attraction? "I like the beer," he told one questioner.

George Romero grew up as a movie-obsessed kid in the Parchester section of the Bronx. At age 14 he was arrested for throwing a dummy off a tenement roof—the climax of an amateur sci-fi epic entitled *The Men From the Meteor.*

One of the investors in *Night of the Living Dead* was a butcher, who was able to supply Romero with all the bones and entrails needed for the film.

The trade paper *Variety* panned *Night of the Living Dead* unmercifully, claiming that it raised "doubts about the future of the regional cinema movement, and about the moral health of filmgoers who cheerfully opt for this unrelieved orgy of sadism . . . amateurism of the first order." Nonetheless, the movie developed a cult following.

PSYCHO (1960)

Psycho, the movie that made half of America scared to get in the shower, was based on the real-life exploits of Ed Gein, whose Wisconsin farmhouse revealed the poorly preserved corpse of Gein's mother as well as evidence of over a dozen murders.

Ed Gein's exploits also made it to the screen in Tobe Hooper's *The Texas Chainsaw Massacre,* in which Gein's acts were reenacted not by a single small-town recluse but by a trio of pathological hillbilly entrepreneurs.

It took 78 separate camera setups to shoot less than a minute of completed footage for *Psycho*'s famous shower scene.

Psycho

In the scene in which her character is murdered in the shower, Janet Leigh's body is not the body actually seen. Leigh was willing to do it, but Hitchcock felt that leading ladies should not have to appear nude and used a double for the body shots.

Anthony Perkins didn't appear in the shower scene either. He was appearing in a play in New York at the time and a double was used for him also.

Although *Psycho*'s shower scene is thought of as "typical Hitchcock," some suggest it wasn't all his idea. It was supposedly conceived by title designer Saul Bass. Hitchcock was responsible for the shots of the blood swirling down the drain, however.

SPOILERS!

Don't Let Anyone Tell You How The Following Movies End. Otherwise you'll be robbed of a special movie-viewing treat the first time you see—

The Sting
Citizen Kane
Psycho
Murder on the Orient Express
The Last of Sheila
Sleuth
The Third Man
Carrie
Butch Cassidy and the Sundance Kid

Do Yourself A Favor. Ask a friend to tell you how each of these movies end. You'll save yourself time and the price of admission on—

The Demon Seed
The Shining
Star Trek—The Motion Picture
The Heavenly Kid
Deathtrap
Friday the 13th (any chapter)

The Musicals

AN AMERICAN IN PARIS (1951)

*D*ancer Cyd Charisse was the number one choice for the female lead in *An American in Paris*, but became pregnant and couldn't do the picture. Remembering a girl he'd seen in a Roland Petit ballet two years earlier, Gene Kelly went to France, located Leslie Caron, and made the 20-year-old dancer into a star.

The final ballet in *An American in Paris* took so long to prepare that director Vincente Minnelli made *Father's Little Dividend* while waiting.

EASTER PARADE (1948)

Vincente Minnelli was set to direct his wife, Judy Garland, in *Easter Parade* when Garland's psychiatrist concluded that it would not help the star's emotional well-being to be directed by Minnelli at that time. Minnelli was replaced by Charles Walters.

Another casualty on *Easter Parade* was Gene Kelly. He was all set to star opposite Garland when he broke his ankle. Kelly told the studio he'd been injured while rehearsing a dance; in fact, he had been playing touch football.

Cyd Charisse was to have her first featured role in *Easter Parade*, but it was not in the stars. Before shooting started she broke her leg and was replaced by Ann Miller.

The wonderful song "We're a Couple of Swells" was written because producer Arthur Freed didn't like the existing number, "Let's Take an Old-Fashioned Walk." It took Irving Berlin only an hour to come up with the replacement, which became one of the high points of the picture.

GIGI (1959)

Although a light musical, *Gigi*, based on a story by Colette, ran into trouble with the censors. The problem? The characters appeared to be anti-marriage.

*F*ilming scenes for *Gigi* at the famous French restaurant Maxim's, cameraman Joe Ruttenberg wanted to cover the mirrors with black drapes to avoid lighting problems. However, the wall of mirrors was the trademark of Maxim's and had to be seen. Ruttenberg eventually put suction cups on lights and stuck them on the ceilings and in other out-of-the-way places so that they wouldn't reflect into the mirrors.

*M*axim's agreed to close for filming, but only for three days and not an hour longer. Since the crew had to shoot two musical numbers as well as several dramatic scenes, the time factor was critical, and it took a lot of pre-planning to complete the scenes in the allotted time.

MARY POPPINS (1964)

*W*hen Julie Andrews received her Oscar for *Mary Poppins* she thanked Jack Warner for his "help"—which had taken the form of making sure she didn't get the role of Eliza in the 1964 movie version of *My Fair Lady*. Warner didn't want to star a screen newcomer as Eliza, and the role went to Audrey Hepburn. So Andrews was free when Disney offered her *Mary Poppins*.

*V*irtually every role in *Mary Poppins* was played by a well-known character actor. The nanny who resigns at the start of the movie was played by Elsa Lanchester, best known as the *Bride of Frankenstein*. The bird woman was played by Jane Darwell—Ma Joad in *The Grapes of Wrath*. Glynis Johns, who played Mrs. Banks, is perhaps best known for introducing the song "Send in the Clowns" in *A Little Night Music* on Broadway. And Ed Wynn made one of his rare screen appearances as the floating Uncle Albert.

The year *Mary Poppins* was released, Dick Van Dyke, who played Bert the chimney sweep, won an Emmy for his highly successful *Dick Van Dyke Show*. He was to win two more Emmys in the two successive years—an impressive three-in-a-row achievement.

ON THE ROAD WITH HOPE & CROSBY & LAMOUR

There were seven films in the famous "Road" series from 1940 to 1962:

Road to Singapore
Road to Zanzibar
Road to Morocco
Road to Utopia
Road to Rio
Road to Bali
The Road to Hong Kong

SINGIN' IN THE RAIN (1952)

Singin' in the Rain was conceived as a showcase/tribute to studio songwriter and producer Arthur Freed, incorporating some of his best songs from the 1920s and 1930s. In order to make them work in a 1952 movie, the story was set in the late 1920s—specifically when sound was revolutionizing the film industry.

All of the sound-related incidents (such as microphones in potted plants or distracting, accidental noises on the soundtrack) were based on real-life horror stories from the era. Screenwriters Betty Comden and Adolph Green turned to MGM's own backlot and talked to the survi-

Singin' in the Rain

vors of the era for first-hand accounts of the early talkies.

*F*or the centerpiece "Singin' in the Rain" number, thousands of gallons of water came from overhead via an elaborate pipe system to simulate rainfall.

THE MUSICAL ROOTS OF SINGIN' IN THE RAIN

* All but two of the songs in the film were originally from early movie musicals. ("Make 'Em Laugh" and "Moses" were newly composed.) In each case, *Singin' in the Rain*'s producer, Arthur Freed, was co-author of the song.

* "Singin' in the Rain" originally appeared in the grand finale of the 1929 MGM film *Hollywood Revue.*

* "Broadway Ballet" actually consisted of two songs: "Broadway Melody" and

"Broadway Rhythm." "Broadway Melody" was from the first MGM talking picture, *Broadway Melody of 1929*. "Broadway Rhythm" was originally done by Eleanor Powell and Frances Langford in *Broadway Melody of 1936*.

* "You Are My Lucky Star" was also from *Broadway Melody of 1936*, and was originally sung by Eleanor Powell.

* "All I Do Is Dream of You" first appeared in the 1943 film *Sadie McKee*, starring Joan Crawford and Gene Raymond.

* "Good Morning" was first presented to the movie public by Mickey Rooney and Judy Garland in the 1939 film *Babes in Arms*.

* All in all, nearly two-thirds of *Singin' in the Rain*'s running time was devoted to singing or musical numbers.

THE WIZARD OF OZ (1939)

Though fondly regarded now, *The Wizard of Oz* took more than a decade to go into the black for MGM. It had been expensive to make and there was not a sufficiently large audience for what was regarded as a children's film.

At first, Buddy Ebsen was to be the Tin Woodsman. But during the course of the filming Ebsen became very ill due to an allergic reaction to the silver paint which covered his body for the role. Jack Haley, then playing the scarecrow, shifted over to the Woodsman (a role he had secretly wanted anyway) and Broadway performer Ray Bolger replaced him as the Scarecrow.

W.C. Fields was originally considered for the role of the Wizard, but he had a disagreement with the studio and was passed over in favor of Frank Morgan.

After filming was completed, the studio made several cuts, including the deletion of an entire dance number, "The Jitterbug." The number did turn up more than four decades later in a compilation film, *That's Dancin'*.

Movies of the Thirties

THE ADVENTURES OF ROBIN HOOD (1938)

The Adventures of Robin Hood was originally developed as a James Cagney vehicle. But Cagney left Warner Bros. in 1935 over a contract dispute and by the time he came back the studio had a new star—Errol Flynn.

Another studio dispute resulted in Errol Flynn's first big hit: Robert Donat walked off *Captain Blood* after an argument with the studio; Flynn got the role and became an instant star.

Chico, California, 350 miles from Los Angeles, provided the forest locations for *The Adventures of Robin Hood*.

The score for *The Adventures of Robin Hood* was the work of Erich Wolfgang Korngold, a serious composer of operas and symphonies. He won an Oscar for his music in this film.

ALL QUIET ON THE WESTERN FRONT (1930)

Erich Maria Remarque's best-seller *All Quiet on the Western Front* was originally intended to be a silent, but after a few weeks of shooting, production was halted and it was redone as a talkie.

Lew Ayres, who became a star after the success of *All Quiet on the Western Front*, was a musician in the orchestra of the popular nightclub Coconut Grove before becoming an actor.

For *All Quiet*, 28 acres of a Southern California ranch were turned into a replica of the German Western Front, and two thousand ex-servicemen were hired as extras.

An ironic bit of casting in *All Quiet:* The dead French soldier with whom the main character, Baumer, shares a foxhole, was played by Raymond Griffith, the brilliant silent comedian whose career was cut short supposedly because his low voice would not record.

At the end of *All Quiet*, Baumer is shot by a sniper as he reaches out for a butterfly. The audience sees only Baumer's hands, and they are the hands not of actor Lew Ayres but of director Lewis Milestone—Ayres had long finished his part in the production by the time Milestone came up with the ending.

In Germany, Nazis picketed theaters and disrupted showings of *All Quiet* by releasing rats and snakes in the theaters. Finally the Berlin censors banned the film for its "demoralizing effect on youth."

FREAKS (1932)

MGM got more than they bargained for when they let Tod Browning make the now legendary *Freaks.* When the studio heads saw Browning's version, they insisted on adding an incongruous, happy ending (which still survives in some prints), and a ludicrous disclaimer assuring audiences that medical science was making obsolete the sort of deformities seen in the film. The studio also took its name off the picture.

All the "freaks" in Browning's film are real people—not actors in makeup. Browning employed several circus freak-show performers, among them dwarfs Harry and Daisy Earles; Siamese twins Daisy and Violet Hilton; Prince Randian the Living Torso; Josephine Joseph, the half-man/half-woman; pinheads Elvira and Jenny Lee Snow; Martha the Armless Wonder; Koo-Koo the Bird Girl; and Lady Olga Barnell, the bearded lady.

Not all the performers who appeared in *Freaks* were pleased with the movie. Lady Olga Barnell, the bearded lady, later denounced the film as "an insult to all freaks."

Some of those who appeared in *Freaks* had moderately successful film careers. Harry Earles had appeared in Tod Browning's 1925 film *The*

Unholy Three, playing a burglar who gets into houses by disguising himself as a baby. The Hilton sisters later starred in *Chained for Life*, a musical (however inappropriate that might seem in view of the subject) about Siamese twins.

Tod Browning knew the world of freaks at first hand. At the age of 16 he had run away from home to join the circus and had toured in carnivals and vaudeville as a barker, contortionist, and blackface comedian.

Variety mistakenly published Tod Browning's obituary in 1944. In fact, the director of *Freaks* lived until 1962, drinking heavily and staying up all night watching old movies on TV. When he died, he left his 1941 Chrysler to his mailman.

GONE WITH THE WIND (1939)

Clark Gable was always a top contender for the part of Rhett Butler in *Gone With the Wind*. For a time, however, producer David O. Selznick toyed with Warner Bros.' offer to lend Erroll Flynn and Bette Davis to star in the film. But MGM, who held Clark Gable's contract, agreed to let Gable do the role when Selznick offered to release the picture through MGM.

Virtually every actress in Hollywood, from Lana Turner to Katharine Hepburn, tested for the part of Scarlett. At one point the choice was narrowed down to Norma Shearer, Jean Arthur, and Paulette Goddard, with Goddard as the favorite. However, Goddard had just married Charles Chaplin and there were indications that the marriage was not legitimate, so to avoid scandal, she was not given the part.

Gone With the Wind

The burning of Atlanta was the first scene to be filmed, and it began without a Scarlett. Facades were used to cover the old Hollywood sets which were then set on fire; stuntmen doubled for the main characters.

It was during the filming of the burning of Atlanta that Selznick's brother Myron, one of Hollywood's leading talent agents, appeared with a woman he introduced as the woman who would play Scarlett O'Hara. She was Vivien Leigh. The nationwide search for Scarlett was over.

The premiere of *Gone With the Wind* was held in Atlanta—appropriately enough—and was attended by Clark Gable, Vivien Leigh, Olivia de Havilland, Evelyn Keyes, and Ona Munson.

One of the leading performers was excluded from the Atlanta premiere. Black actress Hattie McDaniel was present for the festivities but was not allowed into the whites-only theater.

Grand Hotel

GRAND HOTEL (1932)

Grand Hotel was the movie MGM dreaded making. It starred so many major stars that everyone anticipated displays of temperament. One strategy director Edmund Goulding employed for keeping the peace was to make sure that Greta Garbo and Joan Crawford (whom Garbo was convinced would try to steal the picture from her) never appeared in a scene together.

Garbo was one of MGM's biggest stars, and one of the most difficult, but during *Grand Hotel* she was exceptionally hardworking, punctual, and cooperative. The reason? She was very conscious of Joan Crawford as a rising star and was determined to protect her own star status.

IT HAPPENED ONE NIGHT (1934)

It Happened One Night started a movie trend that became known as screwball comedy.

It Happened One Night was based on a short story in *Cosmopolitan* magazine entitled "Night Bus." Director/producer Frank Capra read the story one day at his barber's, and Columbia bought it for $5000.

Capra came up with the title *It Happened One Night*, but the studio didn't like it. Studio head Harry Cohn thought it was too long to fit on the marquee.

Claudette Colbert won the Best Actress Oscar for her role in this film. She hadn't expected to win, and was on her way to New York when she heard the news on the radio. She paused on her way to the station to give the shortest acceptance speech in the history of the Academy: "I'm happy enough to cry, but can't take the time to do it. A taxi is waiting outside and the engine is running."

LOST HORIZON (1937)

Lost Horizon producer/director Frank Capra had difficulty casting the High Lama, who was supposed to be 100 years old. The first two actors cast—A.E. Anson and silent star Henry B. Walthall—both died. So Capra decided to test a younger man who might survive the production. Sam Jaffe, the final choice, was extensively made up to look old. Everything from dry oatmeal to cigarette paper was applied to his face, and eventually a mask of his face was sculpted into that of an old man.

For the early scenes, which take place in the frozen tundra of the Himalayas, Frank Capra used a warehouse with a freezer system used for storing meat. He brought in snow-blowing equipment and constructed an entire set inside the warehouse—where it was so cold that film in the cameras kept jamming until heaters were placed on the film cannisters.

A NIGHT AT THE OPERA (1935)

Following the less-than-spectacular box-office performance of the anarchistic *Duck Soup*, the Marx Brothers had been dropped by Paramount Pictures. At the suggestion of producer Irving Thalberg, MGM picked them up and packaged them with a twist: Their new movies would have more plot, including a love interest.

The formula worked and *A Night at the Opera* was a big success. Ironically, decades later new generations of Marx Brothers fans bemoaned the intrusive love stories and longed for the pure comedy of *Duck Soup*.

It wasn't just the love interest that sold *A Night at the Opera*. The comedy was in top form, honed to perfection as part of a live stage show performed before filming began.

THE FABULOUS MARX BROTHERS ON FILM

First There Were Four: Harpo, Chico, Groucho, and Zeppo

The Cocoanuts (1929)
Animal Crackers (1930)
Monkey Business (1931)
Horse Feathers (1932)
Duck Soup (1933)

Then There Were Three: Harpo, Chico, and Groucho

A Night at the Opera (1935)
A Day at the Races (1937)
Room Service (1938)
At the Circus (1939)
Go West (1940)
The Big Store (1941)
A Night in Casablanca (1946)

And Then There Were Two Plus One: Harpo and Chico, with special guest Groucho

Love Happy (1949)

Movies of the Forties

CASABLANCA (1942)

Casablanca, the enduring Hollywood classic, is based on a play called *Everybody Comes to Rick's*, by Murray Burnett and Joan Alison.

In the original play, Rick Blaine was a married lawyer before he came to Casablanca. In the movie he follows the more exotic occupation of freedom fighter.

The Ingrid Bergman character, Ilsa Lund, was renamed in the film. In the play, she was an American named Lois Meredith. Ann Sheridan, the "Oomph Girl," was considered for the part when the character was still the American Lois.

When the character was changed to a European, Ingrid Bergman became the top contender.

Humphrey Bogart was always top choice for the role of Rick. However, *Casablanca* might have looked quite different if the role of Victor Laszlow had gone not to Paul Henreid but to the producers' first choice—Ronald Reagan.

Although the part was originally written for a man, the makers of *Casablanca* did consider Hazel Scott for the role of Rick's piano-playing friend, Sam. Eventually the role went to Dooley Wilson, whose piano playing was dubbed in the film.

Casablanca started filming without a completed script. Screenwriter Howard Koch would deliver scenes in the morning, as he wrote them, and they'd be shot in the afternoon. Consequently Ingrid Bergman never knew which of the main characters, Laszlo or Rick, she would end up with.

Casablanca

Casablanca won three Oscars—Best Picture, Best Director, and Best Writing (screenplay)—but Ingrid Bergman was a glaring omission from the list of nominations that the film received. She was compensated, however, by receiving a nomination for *For Whom the Bell Tolls* that same year.

CITIZEN KANE (1941)

Before Orson Welles' cinematic masterpiece *Citizen Kane* even appeared on a movie screen, MGM's Louis B. Mayer offered RKO president George Schaefer $842,000 to destroy the picture. By accepting the offer Schaefer would have come out ahead; the move had cost only $686,000 to make. However, he refused.

Before *Citizen Kane* opened, the word was out that the film was a thinly disguised and highly unflattering portrait of publishing magnate William Randolph Hearst. Hearst newspapers refused to carry ads for this or any other RKO movie.

THE GRAPES OF WRATH (1940)

Darryl Zanuck, who bought John Steinbeck's *The Grapes of Wrath* for 20th Century-Fox, used the movie as bait to force Henry Fonda to sign a seven-year contract with Fox—no signature, no starring role. Fonda considered himself a freelancer, but he wanted desperately to play Tom Joad, so he signed.

The Grapes of Wrath is about the Oklahoma "Okies," but location scenes were shot no farther east than Needles, California; the Okie camps were filmed near Pomona.

The Grapes of Wrath

Jane Darwell won an Academy Award for *The Grapes of Wrath.* Henry Fonda was nominated but passed over; his buddy, James Stewart, won that year for *The Philadelphia Story.* The Academy made up for the oversight by awarding Fonda the Oscar for *On Golden Pond*—41 years later.

LAURA (1944)

For a while it seemed that no one except Otto Preminger—who was then out of favor with 20th Century-Fox head Darryl Zanuck—wanted to direct *Laura.* Lewis Milestone, Walter Lang, and John Brahm were among the many who turned it down. Finally Rouben Mamoulian accepted and filmed for 18 days before Zanuck took him off the movie. Stuck with a film but no director, Zanuck finally gave the picture to Preminger.

Dana Andrews desperately wanted to play Mark, the detective in *Laura*, but Zanuck didn't want him. Andrews eventually landed the role by convincing Zanuck's wife, Virginia, that he was right for the part.

The haunting love theme for *Laura* was written by David Raksin, but he had been having difficulty with it until he received a letter from his wife, who wrote that she was leaving him. As the news sank in, Raksin found himself playing the piano. He was playing the theme for *Laura.*

Duke Ellington's "Sophisticated Lady" was Otto Preminger's choice as *Laura*'s theme. It was Raksin who talked Preminger out of it.

Laura

THE MALTESE FALCON (1941)

The leading role of Sam Spade in *The Maltese Falcon* went to Humphrey Bogart only after it had been turned down by George Raft, who considered the project not "an important picture." Edward G. Robinson, Fred MacMurray, and Henry Fonda were also considered for the part.

The Maltese Falcon was originally titled *The Gent From Frisco.*

The part of the fat man, Kasper Gutman, was Sydney Greenstreet's first job in movies.

The ship's captain who delivers the Maltese Falcon to Sam Spade was played by director Huston's father, Walter. The two worked together again in *The Treasure of the Sierra Madre* (1948).

It took 20 takes to film the scene in which Walter Huston, as the ship's captain, delivers the Maltese Falcon to Spade's office. The elder Huston went home exhausted and probably didn't appreciate being called back to do the scene again—especially considering the callback was a joke.

MEET ME IN ST. LOUIS (1944)

When Judy Garland was offered *Meet Me in St. Louis* she initially turned it down. It called for her to play a teenager and Garland felt the time had come for more adult roles. Producer Arthur Freed eventually won her over.

At first Judy Garland and director Vincente Minnelli had a stormy working relationship on *Meet Me in St. Louis.* However, they soon began to date and, though Garland was still married, eventually moved in together. Their later marriage produced a daughter—Liza Minnelli.

Meet Me in St. Louis was too long, but a dispute arose over what to edit out. One potential cut was the Halloween sequence, but Minnelli resisted strenuously—it was this scene that had made him decide to do the picture. Eventually it was agreed that the movie wasn't the same without that scene, so a song called "Boys and Girls Like You and Me" was dropped instead.

THE PHILADELPHIA STORY (1940)

Katharine Hepburn successfully starred on Broadway in *The Philadelphia Story* and had wisely purchased the rights to the play. She sold the rights to MGM only when the studio agreed to let her star in the film.

Hepburn wanted Clark Gable and Spencer Tracy for her male leads in *The Philadelphia Story*. She got James Stewart and Cary Grant instead.

Hepburn had quit her five-year RKO contract in order to play *The Philadelphia Story* on Broadway, leaving behind bad feelings and the label "box-office poison." When the movie opened, critic Bosley Crowther hailed the piece as a "blue-chip comedy" and remarked that if Hepburn was box-office poison then "a lot of people don't read labels."

REBECCA (1940)

Alfred Hitchcock came to America at the invitation of David O. Selznick to do a movie about the *Titanic*. The project fell through and, instead, Hitchcock was given the task of translating to the screen Daphne du Maurier's *Rebecca*.

Hitchcock considered giving a name to the "nameless" heroine of *Rebecca*. His idea was to call her Daphne de Winter—a play on the name of the author of the book.

Rebecca is the only one out of the 51 films Hitchcock made since *The Lodger* (1926) in which he did not make a cameo role. Publicity stills show Hitchcock in costume lurking outside a telephone booth as George Sanders makes a call, but there is no such cameo in the film.

TO HAVE AND HAVE NOT (1944)

To Have and Have Not started out as challenge between director/producer Howard Hawks and writer Ernest Hemingway. The two men were fishing as Hawks tried to convince Hemingway to write for the movies. Hawks claimed that he could make a good movie out of the worst thing that Hemingway ever wrote, even "that piece of junk *To Have and Have Not.*"

Eventually, the two men threw out most of Hemingway's original novel and came up with a completely new story. William Faulkner then came along to write the screenplay, making *To Have and Have Not* the only Hollywood film ever to have two Nobel Prize winners work on it.

To Have and Have Not

To Have and Have Not also marked the beginning of a love-at-first-sight relationship between Humphrey Bogart and Lauren Bacall. Hawks had seen a photo of her in a copy of *Harper's Bazaar* and asked his secretary to find out if she could act. The secretary misunderstood and brought the girl (then named Betty Perske) out to Hollywood.

After polishing Bacall's rough edges, Hawks thought it might be interesting to pair Humphrey Bogart with a girl as tough as he was, so he introduced the two. They ended up making four movies together (*To Have and Have Not, The Big Sleep, Dark Passage,* and *Key Largo*). And in real life they became husband and wife.

Movies of the Fifties

AN AFFAIR TO REMEMBER (1957)

This 1957 classic was made because director Leo McCarey's fortunes were low. Faced with the need for a surefire project, he was drawn back to one of his older films, *Love Affair* (1939), which he remade as *An Affair to Remember.*

For *An Affair to Remember*, the stars of the original version, Charles Boyer and Irene Dunne, were replaced by Cary Grant and Deborah Kerr. Grant was delighted: Years earlier he had visited the set of *Love Affair* and been enthralled with

An Affair to Remember

the script, so he was overjoyed to be cast in the remake.

In the film, Deborah Kerr plays a nightclub singer, but the voice audiences hear is that of Marni Nixon. Nixon sang for Kerr again in the 1956 movie *The King and I.*

The songs in *An Affair to Remember* are the work of one of Hollywood's most prolific tunesmiths, Harry Warren, who numbers among his standards "Chattanooga Choo Choo," "Lullaby of Broadway," and "42nd Street."

THE AFRICAN QUEEN (1951)

The African Queen was originally planned as a vehicle for Elsa Lanchester and her husband, Charles Laughton. Then Bette Davis had hopes of doing it with James Mason. Producer Sam Spiegel, however, thought Humphrey Bogart and Katharine Hepburn, who had never worked together, would make an exciting team. He was right.

ALL ABOUT EVE (1950)

The part of Margo Channing in *All About Eve* was written for Gertrude Lawrence, but she walked off the movie when director Joseph Mankiewicz disapproved of her singing along with the piano on "Liebestraum."

Claudette Colbert was the next choice for the Margo Channing role, but a skiing accident delayed her, and Bette Davis was signed to the role which some believe was her greatest achievement as an actress.

THE CAINE MUTINY (1954)

For *The Caine Mutiny*, it was necessary to borrow some ships, but at first the Navy was not cooperative. They felt the film was un-American and objected to the word "mutiny" in the title. Finally a compromise was reached: The film opens with the introduction, "There has never been a mutiny in the U.S. Navy." The line was worth two destroyers.

Humphrey Bogart wanted so desperately to play Captain Queeg in *The Caine Mutiny* that Columbia, sensing his eagerness, offered him the part at a good salary—but not as good as a star of his magnitude should have been offered. Bogart was furious, but when faced with the take-it-or-leave-it offer, he took it.

FROM HERE TO ETERNITY (1953)

From Here to Eternity was the film they said couldn't be made. In fact, the 1000-page book, with obscene language and frank sex, was turned into a 1950s Hollywood movie by focusing on the love story and changing the prostitutes in the book into hostesses at a "conversation club" on an army base. These and other not so subtle changes helped get the movie past the censor.

It was Clark Gable who suggested Frank Sinatra for the role of Angelo Maggio in *From Here to Eternity*, and Gable even paid Sinatra's airfare back to the States from Africa where Sinatra's wife at the time, Ava Gardner, was filming *Mogambo.* Columbia wanted Eli Wallach instead of Sinatra because Sinatra was thought to be washed up professionally. Sinatra said he would play Maggio for nothing, but after a screen test the studio paid him $10,000 for the part, and Sinatra carried off an Oscar for his performance.

*D*eborah Kerr was not the first choice for the role of Karen Holmes in *From Here to Eternity*. Joan Crawford was cast, but stormed off the set one day. When Kerr said she wanted the role everyone laughed—she was supposedly too high class and refined. It took the producer, the director, and the screenwriter to convince studio heads that she was right for the part.

*T*he famous love scene between Deborah Kerr and Burt Lancaster on the beach was not much fun to make. It was so cold that the two performers had to keep ice cubes under their tongues in order to keep their breath from showing on the screen.

*B*efore *From Here to Eternity*, Donna Reed had spent her time playing "good" characters. She desperately wanted the role of Alma, the hostess in the conversation club. It took three screen tests before director Fred Zinnemann agreed to let her have the part, for which she won the Oscar for Best Supporting Actress.

GIANT (1956)

Director George Stevens had considered Richard Burton for the James Dean role in *Giant*, but Alan Ladd was his first choice. Stevens wished often that Ladd had accepted because he didn't get along with James Dean. The two never had a chance to reconcile their differences, because Dean died in an automobile accident not long after the film was completed.

James Dean's last words in the film were actually spoken by someone else. In the final banquet scene his words were unclear and were supposed to be dubbed, but by the time the dubbing was to be done, Dean was dead.

NORTH BY NORTHWEST (1959)

Originally titled *In a Northerly Direction*, *North by Northwest* was conceived as part of a trilogy, along with *Vertigo* (1958) and *Psycho* (1960).

James Stewart was eager to star in *North by Northwest*, but scriptwriter Ernest Lehman and director/producer Alfred Hitchcock wanted Cary Grant. Unwilling to alienate Stewart, Hitchcock stalled until Stewart signed to do *Bell, Book, and Candle.*

MGM wanted Alfred Hitchcock to cast Cyd Charisse in *North by Northwest*, but in keeping with his predilection for pairing blond women with dark men, Hitchcock chose Eva Marie Saint.

Unimpressed by the dowdy clothes designed for Eva Marie Saint, Alfred Hitchcock took the actress on a shopping spree at Bergdorf Goodman's and chose her clothes for the movie. He even supervised her sophisticated hairdo and makeup.

The famous crop-dusting sequence depicting Indiana farmland was actually shot near Bakersfield, California.

For the Mount Rushmore climax, the presidents' faces were reconstructed in the studio. However, the United States Department of the Interior mandated that the actors could only slide between the faces—there could be no shots of anyone stepping directly on them.

ON THE WATERFRONT (1954)

Henry Cohn, studio head at Columbia, originally offered the part of Terry Malloy in *On the Waterfront* to Frank Sinatra, hoping to capitalize on Sinatra's success in *From Here to Eternity*. When Cohn changed his mind and withdrew the offer, Sinatra sued.

Once Sinatra was out, the part of Terry was offered to Montgomery Clift, who turned it down, calling the Elia Kazan/Budd Schulberg script overblown and corny.

By the time Marlon Brando received his first Academy Award for *On the Waterfront* he had been nominated three times in three successive years—for *A Streetcar Named Desire* in 1951, *Viva Zapata!* in 1952, and *Julius Caesar* in 1953.

On the Waterfront was an outstanding success, receiving eight Oscars including Best Picture, Best Director to Kazan, Best Actor to Brando, and Best Supporting Actress to Eva Marie Saint.

On the Waterfront performers Lee J. Cobb, Rod Steiger, and Karl Malden all received nominations for Best Supporting Actor, but lost to Edmond O'Brien in *The Barefoot Contessa.*

SOME LIKE IT HOT (1959)

The story of two musicians (played by Tony Curtis and Jack Lemmon) who dress up as women to escape a gangster has become a recognized comic masterpiece. However, *Some Like It Hot* also gained quite a reputation because of stories surrounding its leading lady, Marilyn Monroe. She seemed to be playing the real-life role of a temperamental star, rarely on time and available for filming only when she felt like it. Actually she was suffering from depression, and her dependency on chemical stimulants and tranquilizers made her unreliable.

Even when Monroe was on the set, there were problems. She had a tendency to blow her lines, so as many as 20 or 30 takes on a scene were not uncommon. Director Billy Wilder patiently went through take after take after take, until Monroe got the action right.

In one scene, Monroe just couldn't seem to remember the line "Where's the bourbon?" As a solution to the problem, Wilder added a bit, calling for her to open a few drawers in a cabinet. Inside each drawer was a card that read:

"Where's the bourbon?" Monroe then got the scene down by the eighth take.

Tony Curtis had to play his character in three different guises: as a robustly heterosexual leading man, as a guy dressed in drag, and as a sophisticated English millionaire. He had the most fun as the millionaire, deciding that the way to "talk English" was to imitate someone who sounded like a rich, sophisticated Englishman—Cary Grant.

A STAR IS BORN (1954)

A *Star Is Born* was Judy Garland's finest screen role, and also her last major one. Her addiction to weight reducing pills and consequent loss of too many days of rehearsal and filming made studios wary of using her, and she was never entrusted with another major film.

The Judy Garland version of *A Star Is Born* was the third version of this tale of parallel careers—the young starlet on her way up, and her alcoholic husband on his way down. The first version was *What Price Hollywood?*, directed in 1932 by George Cukor who also directed the Garland version. The second version, released in 1937, was also called *A Star Is Born* and starred Janet Gaynor and Frederic March.

Norman Maine's walk into the ocean in *A Star Is Born* was based on an incident in the life of silent screenstar John Bowers, who committed suicide by renting a boat and sailing out to sea.

The final version of *A Star Is Born* ran over three hours, and the studio literally hacked it down to size. It is only recently that the lost portions, including two fine Garland songs, have been restored.

A STREETCAR NAMED DESIRE (1951)

The phenomenal success of the Tennessee Williams play *A Streetcar Named Desire* made it a natural for film. However, the powerful Hollywood standards office raised major objections to the frank and sometimes brutal story, asking for three changes: Blanche's husband could not be homosexual; Blanche could not be a nymphomaniac; and, most important, Blanche could not be raped by Stanley Kowalski.

Tenessee Williams and Elia Kazan (the film's director) agreed to make adjustments to cover the first two points, but refused to eliminate the rape scene. Eventually, the censorship office agreed to a compromise: Blanche would be raped by Stanley, but as a result, Stanley's wife would reject him.

A Streetcar Named Desire

Though this was a blatant reversal on the original stage production, it did mean that Marlon Brando had a very dramatic solo scene to end the film—standing outside mournfully yelling, "Stella! Stella!"

THE TEN COMMANDMENTS (1956)

This was Cecil B. DeMille's final film, and he finished his career at the top and in grand style.

For the film, DeMille spared no expense and shot on location in Egypt. Those on-site arrangements even survived the overthrow of Egypt's President Naguib by Colonel Nasser. The new government even volunteered the Egyptian army to drive the chariots.

The chariot race involved 12,000 people and 1500 animals, and went off without a hitch.

Even a heart problem did not keep Cecil B. DeMille from completing *The Ten Commandments.* While checking an elevated camera position, DeMille blacked out briefly after feeling a stabbing pain in his heart. He was rushed home and told by a doctor not to direct the rest of the film. According to DeMille, he spent the rest of the night praying, woke up feeling fine, and finished the film.

Movies of the Sixties

CASINO ROYALE (1967)

Ian Fleming's first James Bond novel, *Casino Royale*, was part of a different screenplay deal from the other Bond stories. Fleming sold the rights to this one in the 1950s, but the title was not brought to the screen until 1967—when Bond had become an established money-maker.

With Sean Connery so firmly established in the role of Bond, the makers of *Casino Royale* opted to compete by doing a comedy send-up. They cast David Niven as Sir James Bond, the retired "original" Bond who looked askance at the reputation of his current namesake.

The Bond tie-in worked despite the hodge-podge of writers, directors, and stars. *Casino Royale* was one of the top money-makers of 1967, finishing only about six million dollars behind the "official" Bond film of that year, *You Only Live Twice.*

James Bond Films
Starring Sean Connery as Bond

Dr. No. (1962)
From Russia With Love (1963)
Goldfinger (1964)
Thunderball (1965)
You Only Live Twice (1967)
Diamonds Are Forever (1971)
Never Say Never Again (1983)

James Bond Films
Starring Roger Moore as Bond

Live And Let Die (1973)
The Man With The Golden Gun (1974)
The Spy Who Loved Me (1977)
Moonraker (1979)
For Your Eyes Only (1981)
Octopussy (1983)
A View to A Kill (1985)

James Bond Films
Starring George Lazenby as Bond

On Her Majesty's Secret Service (1969)

DR. STRANGELOVE (1964)

Dr. Strangelove, or How I Learned to Stop Worrying and Love the Bomb was originally seen as a serious film, based on Peter George's novel *Red Alert* about the accidental triggering of a nuclear war. The screenwriters found themselves discarding so much material because it *seemed* absurd, that they eventually decided to make the picture a black comedy.

Peter Sellers, playing a triple role in *Dr. Strangelove*, contributed many of his own ideas to his characters, including Strangelove's problems with his mechanical hand and his last-minute resurrection from his wheelchair.

Dr. Strangelove was originally supposed to end with a huge pie fight in the war room. The scene was shot, but then dropped. One of George C. Scott's lines—"Gentlemen, our beloved president has been struck down in the prime of life by a pie!"—seemed tasteless after the recent assassination of John F. Kennedy.

Peter Sellers, who played three roles in *Dr. Strangelove*, was to have played yet another character, Major T.J. "King" Kong, the redneck bomber pilot. However, a hip injury prevented him from taking on a fourth role and Slim Pickens did it instead.

GOLDFINGER (1964)

Goldfinger introduced the first of the Bond supercars, the silver Aston Martin DB-5 (initialed for its designer, David Brown). The success led to the Lotus car-submarine, the portable helicopter "Little Nellie," and the Astrojet.

The Aston Martin in *Goldfinger* had several clever features, including exhaust pipes that squirted oil to discourage tailgating. Originally tacks were to be discharged instead of oil, but someone suggested that children might copy the

Goldfinger

idea and bring about an international epidemic of flat tires.

The idea of murdering a person by covering the body with gold paint was originally used in the 1946 Boris Karloff movie *Bedlam*. When Shirley Eaton was painted gold in *Goldfinger*, however, a six-inch square of her abdomen was left unpainted in order that she not be sacrificed for her art.

Gert Frobe, playing the evil Goldfinger, had such a thick German accent that his voice had to be dubbed throughout the film.

Sean Connery's salary for *Dr. No* was around $45,000 and didn't increase appreciably for *From Russia With Love*. By the third Bond movie, *Goldfinger*, Connery was ready for a raise, but the producers balked. However, when Connery injured his back during the Fort Knox sequence in which Oddjob (Harold Sakata) throws him against the wall, Connery took a couple of days off and let it be known that he wasn't coming back to work until he got a raise. He then got his raise.

For his seventh (and most recent) Bond, *Never Say Never Again*, Sean Connery reportedly earned $5 million up front and a healthy percent of the gross. Not bad for playing, as Dr. No said, "a stupid policeman."

THE GRADUATE (1967)

Dustin Hoffman, star of *The Graduate*, wasn't everyone's idea of a potential movie hero. Hoffman's Aunt Pearl once told him, "You can't be an actor. You're not good-looking enough."

An early stage appearance by Dustin Hoffman didn't go over too well with his backers. In seventh grade he played the role of Tiny Tim in *A Christmas Carol* and, accepting a dare from a ninth grader, broke up the audience with the line, "God bless us everyone, goddamit." This piece of improvisational theater got him suspended.

Dustin Hoffman was named for another movie performer—silent screen cowboy Dustin Farnum.

Dustin Hoffman studied at the Pasadena Playhouse where he was told he would definitely make it in movies—in ten or fifteen years.

The Graduate earned Dustin Hoffman $17,000—and an Oscar nomination (he lost to Rod Steiger).

WHO'S AFRAID OF VIRGINIA WOOLF? (1966)

At first, Richard Burton turned down the role of husband George in the planned film version of Edward Albee's intense stage play. One reason was that he was afraid the hostility on the screen between George and his wife Martha (to be played by Elizabeth Taylor) would spill over into their own real-life marriage.

Elizabeth Taylor convinced Burton to do the part and his worst fears did not come true. In fact, the opposite took place. The two stars found that after venting their anger in the film, they did not have time or energy for such hostilities at home.

This drama about a bickering college town couple (named after George and Martha Washington) won Oscars for supporting actress Sandy Dennis and for Elizabeth Taylor (as Best Actress).

Richard Burton, however, lost the Best Actor Oscar to Paul Scofield in that year's Best Picture, *A Man for All Seasons.* At the awards ceremony, Taylor quite bluntly declared that it was nice to win but that, "the edge was taken off because Richard didn't win, and he was the best actor of the year."

Movies of the Seventies & Eighties

ANNIE HALL (1977)

One suggested title for the Woody Allen movie *Annie Hall* was *Anhedonia*—which means an inability to experience pleasure.

A lot of material in Woody Allen's *Annie Hall* never made it to the screen. Scenes were cut when Allen and his editor, Ralph Rosenblum, decided to concentrate on one major aspect of the story: the romance between Alvy and Annie.

One of the scenes cut from *Annie Hall* is a nightmare sequence in which Alvy is captured by Nazis. He refuses to talk until threatened with execution, then pulls out a hand puppet and gives the information ventriloquially.

Also never seen in *Annie Hall:* a fantasy sequence in which Alvy's trip to Los Angeles turns into a parody of *Invasion of the Body Snatchers*—Alvy and Annie are in danger of turning into Californians overnight.

APOCALYPSE NOW (1979)

Frances Ford Coppola's ill-fated *Apocalypse Now* was supposed to be shot for $12 million in 16 weeks. In fact, the budget ballooned to $31,500,000 and shooting dragged on for over a year.

More than 1,100,000 feet of film were exposed for *Apocalypse Now.*

For the "Ride of the Valkyries" air attack, 1200 gallons of gasoline were burnt in 90 seconds to simulate a napalm drop. The 90-second climax to the Do Lung Bridge scene consumed over 500 smoke bombs, 100 phosphorus sticks, another 1200 gallons of gasoline, 1750 sticks of dynamite, 5000 feet of detonating cord, and 2000 rockets, flares, and tracers.

CHARIOTS OF FIRE (1981)

Chariots of Fire scriptwriter Colin Welland advertised in British papers for anyone who had reminiscences of the 1924 Olympics. As a result, runner Aubrey Montague's son sent Welland his father's letters, and these became the basis of the movie's narration, which was told through Aubrey's character (played by Nicholas Farrell).

In the film, Scottish runner Eric Liddell's sister Jennie is shown as having stood in the way of his running, when in truth she had no such objection. Nor did she attend the 1924 Olympics to see her brother win. Both incidents were included for the benefit of the plot.

Chariots of Fire was director Hugh Hudson's first movie (he had previously made documentaries and commercials). It was also a first for the two principal actors, Ben Cross, who played Harold Abrahams, and Ian Charleson, who played Eric Liddell.

To familiarize himself with the character of runner Eric Liddell, who ran for the glory of God, Ian Charleson read the Bible from cover to cover.

Ben Cross, preparing to play Harold Abrahams, hired a coach to help him with his running, and studied the character of Abrahams so thoroughly that his wife complained, "I thought I married a crazy Irish actor. Why am I living with a crazy Jewish athlete?"

DIRTY HARRY (1971)

Clint Eastwood was not the first actor to be offered the role of police inspector Harry Callahan in *Dirty Harry*. Paul Newman had already turned down the role because he considered the character too tough.

Eastwood agreed to do *Dirty Harry* if he could get his friend Don Siegel at Universal to produce and direct. Thus Siegel returned to the Warner lot after a 22-year absence.

THE GODFATHER (1972)

Although Marlon Brando was the first choice of both author and co-scenarist Mario

Puzo and director Francis Ford Coppola for the role of Don Corleone in *The Godfather*, Paramount wouldn't consider him at first. They thought Brando was washed up and hard to control. Finally they agreed to consider Brando on three conditions: that he take no salary, that he submit to a screen test, and that he personally finance any budget overruns due to his own antics. It was hardly an offer he couldn't refuse, but Brando accepted.

KRAMER VS. KRAMER (1979)

Dustin Hoffman originally turned down the leading role in *Kramer vs. Kramer*, but agreed to do it after being promised that he could collaborate with writer/director Robert Benton on developing the character. Ironically, the movie depicted a man going through an untidy divorce just at the time Hoffman's marriage to dancer Anne Byrne was breaking up.

It was rumored that Dustin Hoffman accepted the part in *Kramer vs. Kramer* so that Al Pacino wouldn't get it. The story—though totally unfounded—became a running gag on the set. The crew even gave Hoffman a coffee mug with Pacino's name on it.

Kate Jackson was the first choice for the part of Mrs. Kramer, but was committed to TV's *Charlie's Angels* and couldn't accept. The role went to Meryl Streep, and she won a Best Supporting Actress Oscar for her efforts.

LAST TANGO IN PARIS (1973)

In a 4000-word rave notice in *The New Yorker*, critic Pauline Kael compared the debut of

Last Tango in Paris

Last Tango in Paris at the New York Film Festival to the premiere of Stravinsky's *Rites of Spring*. The review was reprinted in its entirety across two pages of *The New York Times* as part of the ad campaign by the film's distributor, United Artists.

*D*ominique Sanda was to have taken the female lead in *Last Tango in Paris* but became pregnant, as did her replacement, Catherine Deneuve. The role then went to unknown actress Maria Schneider, whom director Bernardo Bertolucci described as "a Lolita—but more perverse."

*S*eeking a replacement actor for Jean-Louis Trintignant, director Bernardo Bertolucci was reminded of Marlon Brando when he saw some paintings by British artist Francis Bacon with their "images of despair." One of the paintings appears in the film's credit sequence.

*B*rando improvised most of his own lines,

giving what many consider his last great performance.

The Catholic church in Italy condemned *Last Tango;* the film was banned for two months, and later banned permanently. All prints were seized and the negative burned. But director Bernardo Bertolucci had made duplicate negatives.

M*A*S*H (1970)

Over a dozen directors were approached to do *M*A*S*H* and all gave the subject a thumbs down. In desperation the studio, 20th Century-Fox, turned to a young filmmaker with only a couple of films to his credit. Taking a major chance, they gave the job to the young Robert Altman.

*M*A*S*H* originated as a book by Richard Hooker, which is the pseudonym of a doctor who had served during the Korean war.

*M*A*S*H* is an acronym for Mobile Army Surgical Hospital.

*M*A*S*H* is one of the few films to have the closing credits spoken out loud: They are announced over the P.A. system.

Gary Burghoff, who played Radar O'Reilly, was the only performer featured in both the movie and TV versions of *M*A*S*H*.

It is ironic that Ring Lardner, Jr. won an Oscar for the screenplay of *M*A*S*H* because director Altman virtually abandoned Lardner's script, preferring to have the actors improvise.

ROCKY (1976)

Sylvester Stallone got the idea for a movie about an underdog boxer from watching a match between Mohammed Ali and Chuck Wepner on TV. Wepner surprised everyone by lasting the entire bout against odds-on favorite Ali, inspiring Stallone to write the script for *Rocky*.

Sylvester Stallone wrote the script in three days and was offered $75,000 for it by producers Irwin Winkler and Robert Chartoff. Incredibly, he turned them down. He wouldn't sell unless he could star in the film. They wanted the script so badly that they agreed.

Rocky was Frank Capra's favorite movie of 1976—it was the sort of rags-to-riches story that Capra had been so fond of directing himself.

TAXI DRIVER (1976)

Director Martin Scorsese was responsible for a daring bit of casting for *Taxi Driver*, selecting 12-year-old Jodie Foster to play the role of preteen prostitute Iris.

Previously, Foster had appeared in several television shows and three movies for Disney Productions, as well as Scorsese's *Alice Doesn't Live Here Anymore*. Nonetheless, she was hesitant about the character, believing the part better suited to an older performer.

Foster's mother, a former Hollywood press agent, talked her daughter into taking the part, chiefly because she liked the idea of Jodie working again with Scorsese and actor Harvey Keitel

Taxi Driver

(who had also been in *Alice Doesn't Live Here Anymore*).

*M*any precautionary steps were taken to ensure that Foster could handle her role. Foster was interviewed by a psychiatrist to establish her maturity and stability; representatives of the child welfare board viewed each day's rushes to protect Foster from any psychological trauma; and Foster's 20-year-old sister, Connie, replaced her in certain scenes.

*J*odie Foster was fine after the movie, though there was one aftereffect that was impossible to foresee. John Hinckley, who attempted to assassinate President Ronald Reagan, later publicly declared his love for Foster, whom he had seen in *Taxi Driver*.

FROM SILVER SCREEN TO HOME SCREEN

A baker's dozen of films given subsequent TV series treatment (feature film date/TV series starting date):

Barefoot in the Park (1967/1970)
Casablanca (1942/1955 & 1983)
Flamingo Road (1949/1981)
Foul Play (1978/1981)
Going My Way (1944/1962)
House Calls (1978/1979)
King's Row (1941/1955)
Love Is a Many Splendored Thing (1955/1967)
*M*A*S*H* (1970/1972)
The Odd Couple (1968/1970)
Operation Petticoat (1959/1977)
Seven Brides for Seven Brothers (1954/1982)
Voyage to the Bottom of the Sea (1961/1964)

FACTS ABOUT THE TV SHOWS

Talk Shows & Quiz Shows

THE ED SULLIVAN SHOW/TOAST OF THE TOWN (1948-71)

*T*welve days after Milton Berle first appeared on NBC with *Texaco Star Theater*, Ed Sullivan introduced his first "really big show" for CBS, *Toast of the Town*.

*U*nlike Berle, Ed Sullivan was not a performer. He was selected to host the show because he had a keen eye for talent. Sullivan did not disappoint CBS. On the first program, he introduced home audiences to the zany comedy of Dean Martin and Jerry Lewis (paid $200 for their appearance), and the music of pianist Eugene List.

*H*umorist Fred Allen explained: "Ed Sullivan will stay on television as long as other people have talent."

*S*ullivan's most famous "first" came on February 9, 1964, when he helped turn the entertainment industry on its head with the words, "Here are the Beatles!" That night millions of teenagers got their first look at the Fab Four from Liverpool performing live.

The Beatles on The Ed Sullivan Show

THE TONIGHT SHOW (1954-)

The Tonight Show began its late night run on NBC with Steve Allen as host. He carried on with such regulars as Gene Rayburn, Steve Lawrence, Eydie Gorme, Don Knotts, and Tom Poston.

Jack Paar took over the slot in 1957. His regulars included Hugh Downs, Dodi Goodman, and Cliff Arquette as Charley Weaver.

The Tonight Show

Johnny Carson began his stint on the program on October 2, 1962. Since then, he has spent more time in the host's chair then all the previous hosts, guest hosts, and substitute hosts combined . . . except on Mondays, of course.

LATE NIGHT WITH DAVID LETTERMAN (1982-)

David Letterman's show is one of those series that seems tailor-made for a late night timeslot. He has found a faithful audience that is enthralled with his sarcastic, in-joke approach to the world of television.

Letterman enjoys taking the camera out of the studio—and even out of the RCA building in New York. Letterman tapes his show at about 5:00 P.M. (EST) each day, so there is always plenty of foot traffic.

Letterman invites viewers to bring their animals onto the show for "Stupid Pet Tricks" (complete with videotaped "Instant Replays").

Late Night With David Letterman

The routine later spawned "Stupid Human Tricks."

When Letterman learned that Phil Donahue was changing the location of his daily program from Chicago to New York City, he immediately launched a "Donahue Countdown," which included a huge backdrop calendar with each passing day crossed off. This culminated in a visit by Donahue himself, who confessed amazement at the entire event—and was delighted at all the free publicity.

THE $64,000 QUESTION (1955-58)

The $64,000 Question was the series that started the mad rush for big-money quiz show programming in the mid-1950s. The series became an instant hit shortly after it premiered in the summer of 1955.

Contestants on *The $64,000 Question* were "ordinary people" who happened to be experts in one particular area, which they chose as their subject while competing on the program. To increase the onscreen drama, they were placed in see-through isolation booths on stage as they drew nearer to the final big-money questions.

Successful contestants on *The $64,000 Question* included Dr. Joyce Brothers (in the category of boxing), Bronx cab driver Gino Prato (in the category of opera), and Marine Captain Richard S. McCutchen (the first to win $64,000—his category was gastronomy).

There was even a spin-off show for alumni of *The $64,000 Question*, *The $64,000 Challenge*. This opportunity for a double score allowed Teddy Nadler to become one of the biggest winners in television game-show history. Winnings for his appearances on both series came to more than $260,000.

YOU BET YOUR LIFE (1950-61)

When Groucho Marx brought his successful quiz show format to television in 1950, he merely added a camera to what he had been doing on radio for three years.

Though set up as a quiz program, *You Bet Your Life* was really a showcase for the wit and gibes of Groucho Marx. On radio and in the early days of the television series, Groucho would film (and tape) about an hour's worth of material for the eventual half-hour show. This allowed unsuccessful (or overly risqué) exchanges to be edited out of the final broadcast version.

Groucho obviously knew a little bit about the contestants before they came out (such as unusual sounding names that he was sure to make fun of), but otherwise the exchanges were unrehearsed and spontaneous.

Each show featured a "secret word" which, if spoken by one of the contestants, would result in an extra $100. It was "a common word, something you see every day." At first, a duck doll would be lowered from the ceiling showing the secret word. In later years, a beautiful woman would often be lowered instead.

Speaking for a generation of baby boomers, Dick Cavett noted in his introduction to "An Evening With Groucho" (a live stage presentation at New York's Carnegie Hall in 1972), that he knew Groucho *first* from the television show, then from the Marx Brothers films.

Humor & Variety Shows

THE RICHARD PRYOR SHOW (1977)

Richard Pryor was host to a limited run variety series for NBC that was perversely slotted in an early-evening time period. With Pryor's reputation for explicit language and controversial material, this practically guaranteed a collision with the network censors. It happened with the opening scene of the first show.

The Richard Pryor Show

When the program aired, all that the viewers saw was a full-screen caption that the beginning of *The Richard Pryor Show* would not be seen—ever! The scene that had been cut started as a tight close-up on Pryor, who began to explain that he did not have to "give up anything" to do a program on network television. The camera then pulled back to a full-body view, revealing an apparently castrated Pryor. Actually, he was just wearing a skin-tight body stocking.

Both the network and Pryor agreed to give up the series after about a month. Even with the network limitations, though, the series was actually good, and, in terms of controversial and topical comedy, can be seen as a forerunner of *Saturday Night Live*, with a good supporting cast and excellent skits and characterizations by Pryor.

SATURDAY NIGHT LIVE (1975-)

The opening skit of the very first show set up the trademark punchline, "Live from New York, it's *Saturday Night!*"

In the first scene, Michael O'Donoghue played the part of someone attempting to teach an immigrant some English. John Belushi played the pupil who imitated everything his teacher said or did.

When he saw the teacher keel over from a heart attack, the pupil faithfully followed him to the floor, dead. Chevy Chase, playing a stage-hand, came over to the bodies, looked at them, then at the camera, and ironically pronounced them: "Live, from New York!"

In the first season, the regular cast was dubbed "The Not Ready for Prime Time Players." They included: Dan Aykroyd, John Belushi,

Saturday Night Live

Chevy Chase, Jane Curtin, Garrett Morris, Laraine Newman, and Gilda Radner.

After Chevy Chase left the series, Bill Murray stepped into the main cast.

THE SMOTHERS BROTHERS COMEDY HOUR (1967-75)

The Smothers Brothers Comedy Hour first made its mark by doing what no other CBS show had been able to do for years—it pushed competing *Bonanza* (on NBC) out of the number-one slot. Very soon thereafter, though, the program became known as the most controversial show on television.

Eventually, despite their good ratings, *The Smothers Brothers Show* was canceled, chiefly because of the brothers' insistence on topical skits and guests. During their time, however, they presented some classic moments in television comedy.

During the 1968 political campaign, regular Pat Paulsen staged a mock run for the presidency as a member of the Straight Talking American Government (STAG) Party.

Guest comedian David Steinberg appeared delivering tongue-in-cheek sermons, while regular Bob Einstein appeared as the stone-faced Officer Judy.

Tom and Dick Smothers also had their share of contemporary rock acts as guests, including The Doors, Simon and Garfunkel, The Who, and (in an impromptu cameo) George Harrison.

TEXACO STAR THEATER/MILTON BERLE SHOW (1948-56)

Milton Berle was television's first superstar. As host of NBC's Tuesday night *Texaco Star Theater* (beginning in 1948), Berle's vaudeville-style slapstick humor inspired millions of people to purchase their first television sets.

At first, Berle was considered only one of several possible permanent hosts for the program. He appeared for two months, then a rotating group of emcees took over (including Henny Youngman, Morey Amsterdam, and George Price). But only Berle generated that special excitement.

Very quickly, Milton Berle earned a number of nicknames, including the obvious "Mr. Television" and the affectionate "Uncle Miltie."

Berle practically owned Tuesday nights until the mid-1950s. Perhaps the most unusual competition he faced was from God, in the form of the heartfelt talks by Roman Catholic Bishop Fulton J. Sheen on *Life Is Worth Living* on the DuMont network.

Berle finally lost out to the growing popularity of filmed series, being edged out in his time slot by both *Cheyenne* (a filmed western) and *You'll Never Get Rich* (a filmed sitcom).

TURN-ON (1969)

Though thousands of series have been canceled since the beginning of television, *Turn-On* entered the record books as one of the most famous flops in TV history. It ran just one night:

Wednesday, February 5, 1969, on ABC. Due to the time difference between the east and west coasts, the program was essentially canceled before it even aired in California.

Turn-On was meant to be a free-wheeling comedy-variety show, in the style of *Rowan and Martin's Laugh-In*. It was even produced by the same person, George Schlatter. But while *Laugh-In* mixed a variety of comedy styles into a fast-paced format (including old-fashioned, stand-up routines by Dan Rowan and Dick Martin), *Turn-On* merely presented one joke after another at breakneck speed.

A computer acted as host for the show, assisted by a guest celebrity. Tim Conway was the guest in the one and only broadcast. There were several more episodes in the can, but they never aired.

One problem with *Turn-On* was that some viewers and network affiliates judged the show to be not only bad (most of the jokes fell flat), but in bad taste as well. Taking no chances, ABC replaced *Turn-On* with the wholesome musical variety show *The King Family*.

FRIDAY NIGHT VIDEOS (1983-)

With MTV available only to cable subscribers, NBC decided that a program exclusively devoted to popular rock videos could be a big hit. The network was right.

Friday Night Videos was, in some ways, even better than MTV. Viewers with only a casual interest in the form could catch the best of the current productions in one weekly 90-minute segment, rather than trying to spot them on 24-hour cable service.

Friday Night Videos was the first television program to break with the practice of running the rock videos without paying anything to the companies that provided them. Instead, *Friday Night Videos* established and paid a standard "production fee."

Though *Friday Night Videos* obviously could not compete with MTV in the number and frequency of the videos shown, the program did work on its own specials and exclusives. The most unusual was the first-ever joint interview with Paul McCartney and Julian Lennon. This came about as a happy "accident": Two individual interviews were scheduled to be taped in New York City very close together so that if there were any delays, the two stars would find themselves in front of the cameras together. There were and they did.

Kids' Shows

THE ADVENTURES OF SUPERMAN (1951-57)

The syndicated *Superman* series first appeared in 1953 as an effective but low-budget adventure program. Though the footage of Superman in flight or crashing through walls was usually quite effective, for the most part there were few elaborate special effects. Generally, the

The Adventures of Superman

extremely likable cast carried the audience's interest and identification.

In its first year of production, the *Superman* schedule was so hectic that parts of several episodes were filmed at the same time. As a result, the main characters (Clark Kent, Lois Lane, Jimmy Olsen, and Perry White) were usually seen in the same clothes week after week after week.

By 1954, *Superman* episodes were being filmed in color, even though mass acceptance of color television was more than a decade away.

Phyllis Coates played Lois Lane in the first 26 episodes of the series. Thereafter, Noel Neill took over the role. Oddly, Neill had played Lois *before* Coates, appearing in the 15-episode theatrical serial, *Superman vs. the Atomic Man.*

The Adventures of Superman did not come to network television until 1957, when ABC began running episodes as part of its weekday afternoon schedule.

THE ALVIN SHOW (1961-62)

During the early 1960s, a rash of half-hour cartoon programs hit prime-time television, chiefly on ABC (*Bugs Bunny, The Flintstones, The Jetsons*, and *Top Cat*).

The Alvin Show was set up as a cartoon comedy-variety show (like *Bugs Bunny*), with the three singing Chipmunks (Simon, Theodore, and Alvin) introducing segments as well as starring in them.

Songwriter Ross Bagdasarian (under the name David Seville) did the voices for the characters, just as he had done in a series of novelty records by The Chipmunks—beginning with "The Chipmunk Song" (a humorous Christmas single) back in 1958.

Bagdasarian used speeded up vocal tracks of his own voice to provide the singing sound of Simon, Theodore, and Alvin. He had used that same trick for a previous novelty rock record, "The Witch Doctor."

The Alvin Show also featured a non-Chipmunk segment starring Clyde Crashcup, inventor of everything, and his assistant, Leonardo. Shepard Menken supplied the voice for Crashcup.

BATMAN (1966-68)

Producer William Dozier considered dozens of candidates for the role of the dramatic voice-over narrator for *Batman*. He needed someone who could deliver just the right tone of mock seriousness while asking such burning questions

Batman

as: "Is this the *end* for the Dynamic Duo?" Eventually William Dozier decided the man best suited for the job was William Dozier.

Batman was staged as a classic cliff-hanger, with each story usually presented in two parts. In its first two seasons, the program aired twice a week on ABC (Wednesday and Thursday nights), so viewers of episode one inevitably returned the next night for the solution ("Same Bat-Time! Same Bat-Channel!").

Gadgets were the stock-in-trade of the show. Perhaps the most popular was the supercharged Batmobile, a fully functioning turbo-powered racing car. Long after *Batman* ended its run, the Batmobile was still being displayed at auto shows around the world.

BATMAN AND ROBIN'S FANTASTIC FOES

During the two-year run of *Batman*, these were some of the performers who turned up as guest villains against the Caped Crusaders.

* *The Riddler*, played by Frank Gorshin and later by John Astin
* *The Penguin*, played by Burgess Meredith
* *Zelda the Great*, played by Anne Baxter
* *Mr. Freeze*, played by George Sanders and later by Otto Preminger, then by Eli Wallach
* *The Mad Hatter*, played by David Wayne
* *The Joker*, played by Cesar Romero
* *Catwoman*, played by Julie Newmar and later by Eartha Kitt
* *King Tut*, played by Victor Buono
* *The Bookworm*, played by Roddy McDowall
* *The Archer*, played by Art Carney
* *The Minstrel*, played by Van Johnson
* *Ma Parker*, played by Shelley Winters
* *The Clock King*, played by Walter Slezak
* *Egghead*, played by Vincent Price
* *Chandell the pianist*, played by Liberace
* *Marsha, Queen of Diamonds*, played by Carolyn Jones
* *Shame*, played by Cliff Robertson
* *The Puzzler*, played by Maurice Evans
* *The Black Widow*, played by Tallulah Bankhead
* *The Siren*, played by Joan Collins
* *Louie the Lilac*, played by Milton Berle
* *Lord Phogg*, played by Rudy Vallee
* *Nora Clavicle*, played by Barbara Rush
* *Cassandra*, played by Ida Lupino
* *Minerva*, played by Zsa Zsa Gabor

ROCKY AND HIS FRIENDS (1959-64)

The adventures of Rocky the Flying Squirrel and Bullwinkle the Moose began as an afternoon cartoon series for ABC in the fall of 1959. The network soon added a late Sunday afternoon show as well.

Each half-hour show opened and closed with the cliff-hanger adventures of Rocky and Bullwinkle. In between, they as well as other characters appeared in various skits and segments such as "Bullwinkle's Corner," "Fractured Fairy Tales," and "Mr. Know-It-All."

The first story focused on a secret rocket formula and went on for months. Bill Scott, the voice of Bullwinkle, explained that there was a very good reason for the meandering nature of the tale—they really didn't know how long the new series was going to be. So they just kept on going with the plot.

The most famous pun on the show was something called the Kurwood Derby, a play on the name Durward Kirby (sidekick to comedy-variety star Garry Moore and co-host of *Candid Camera*). It stuck so well that for years people referred to Kirby himself as "Derwood" Kirby. When *Rocky and His Friends* went into rerun sydication, those episodes were not included in the package.

Beginning in 1961 (with a shift in networks), the title of the program was changed to *The Bullwinkle Show*, reflecting the fact that the moose was actually the most popular character on the show.

Law & Order

BARNEY MILLER (1975-82)

New York's 12th Precinct was the setting for this "cop-house" sitcom. In each episode, there would be two or three cases going on at the same time, along with the personal interaction among the detectives.

Hal Lindon played Captain Barney Miller. Abe Vigoda was Detective Phil Fish, somewhat ironic casting because previously Vigoda had played a ruthless Mafia leader in the feature film *The Godfather* (1972).

Ron Glass played Ron Harris, an aspiring author who turned the precinct routine into the basis for his first novel, *Blood on the Badge.*

Steve Landesberg played Arthur Dietrich, the glib, articulate detective who seemed to know a little bit about everything.

Jack Soo played Nick Yemana, the detective who had a weakness for betting on the horses, and, even worse, made terrible coffee.

Maxwell Gail played Stanley ("Wojo") Wojohowicz, the precinct's broad-shouldered, kind-hearted Polish detective.

For one season, Gregory Sierra played Chano Amenguale, a fiery Puerto Rican detective.

CAGNEY AND LACY (1982-   )

This story of two female police detectives first ran in 1981 as a made-for-TV movie starring Tyne Daley as Mary Beth Lacey and Loretta Swit as Chris Cagney. With *M*A*S*H* still running at the time, Swit was unable to continue her role in a follow-up series, so the part went to Meg Foster.

Cagney and Lacey had a brief run in the spring of 1982 and was picked up by CBS for the fall. However, the network wanted the part of Chris Cagney recast. So the producers turned to Sharon Gless, whom they had previously considered for the role.

The series attracted marginal ratings, so CBS canceled it in 1983—only to be hit with a barrage of protest letters and critical articles. In response, the network renewed it for a limited number of episodes that had to score well, and by 1984 *Cagney and Lacy* was a popular and critical success.

COLUMBO (1968-78)

The character of homocide detective Lieutenant Columbo (played by Peter Falk) was introduced in a 1968 made-for-TV movie, *Prescription: Murder.*

In that film, creators Richard Levinson and William Link set up the *Columbo* formula: The deceptively disorganized and disheveled detective ever-so-slowly and methodically chips away at the alibi of the self-assured murderer (played by Gene Barry in the original film).

When NBC and Universal Studios decided to turn it into a series, they asked Levinson and Link for a new pilot film. After pointing out that *Prescription: Murder* was a perfectly good pilot film, they produced another one anyway, called *Ransom for a Dead Man*, with Lee Grant as the confident killer.

The first episode of the regular *Columbo* series was called "Murder by the Book." It was directed by Steven Spielberg and written by Steven Bochco. Jack Cassidy played one-half of a successful mystery writing team who killed his co-author.

One of the in-jokes in "Murder by the Book" was the title of one of the books co-authored by Cassidy's character. The title was *Prescription: Murder*—the name of the original *Columbo* feature-film pilot.

Throughout the entire run of the series, Peter Falk wore the same battered trench coat. *Columbo* thus earned the distinction of being

Columbo

Miami Vice

the hit series with the least expensive wardrobe for its star.

HILL STREET BLUES (1981-)

Hill Street Blues was one of the lowest rated series in modern television history to be picked up for a second season. There were two key reasons for its renewal by NBC: The program had received strong critical praise and seemed a worthwhile show strictly for prestige reasons; and, at the time, NBC had very few successful shows, so it made more sense to hold onto a critical smash that could find an audience rather than to launch yet another unknown series.

Steven Bochco and Michael Kozoll, the creators of *Hill Street Blues*, emphasized character interaction and a gritty, realistic atmosphere. In that spirit, one of the most unusual plotlines involved the death of one of the characters, Sergeant Phil Esterhaus (who did roll call), when the actor who played him (Michael Conrad) died. The plotline was carried on for several months, ending with the cremation of Esterhaus and the spreading of his ashes in the Hill Street precinct area.

MIAMI VICE (1984-)

Legend has it that NBC President Grant Tinker wrote a two-word description of what he wanted in a new TV cop show: "MTV cops." *Miami Vice* fit the bill perfectly.

Miami Vice was a police series done with an eye on style and presentation, especially with the costumes and accompanying music. Sometimes, like a rock video that might run on MTV, there was an appropriate song playing behind the action. Most of the time, there were bits of songs or flashy instrumentals that helped punctuate the action.

Like MTV, *Miami Vice* provided a special boost to the music and musicians it featured. In the first season, former member of The Eagles Glenn Frey scored a hit with the song "Smuggler's Blues" when it was used as the cornerstone for an entire episode. Frey also played a part in that episode.

PERRY MASON (1957-66)

Erle Stanley Gardner created the character of Perry Mason in a series of top-selling murder

Perry Mason

mysteries. For the television version, Raymond Burr portrayed the no-nonsense defense attorney, though, ironically, he had originally tested for the role of prosecuting attorney Hamilton Burger, eventually played by William Talman.

The two essential supporting players on Perry's team included his efficient private secretary Della Street (Barbara Hale) and private detective Paul Drake (William Hopper, son of Hollywood columnist Hedda Hopper).

In the last episode of the series, "The Case of the Final Fadeout," Erle Stanley Gardner himself played the judge, and a few other behind-the-scenes production people were cast as various suspects and witnesses.

There was an unsuccessful remake of the series in 1973, with Monte Markham as Mason. That series lasted barely four months.

77 SUNSET STRIP (1958-64)

Efrem Zimbalist, Jr. starred as detective Stuart Bailey who operated out of the swank offices at 77 Sunset Strip in Hollywood. Roger Smith played his partner, Jeff Spencer.

Edd Byrnes played Gerald Lloyd Kookson III, better known as "Kookie," the parking lot attendant next door at Dino's. Kookie was quite popular as a teen sex symbol and Byrnes even had a hit record in 1959 called "Kookie, Kookie, Lend Me Your Comb" (sung by Connie Stevens).

The success of *77 Sunset Strip* inspired Warner Bros. to launch a number of other hour-

77 Sunset Strip

long action-adventure series, including *Surfside 6*, *Hawaiian Eye*, *Bourbon Street Beat*, and *The Alaskans.*

NUMBER ONE SHOWS 1950-1984

Texaco Star Theater (1949-51)
Arthur Godfrey's Talent Scouts (1951-52)
I Love Lucy (1952-55; 1956-57)
The $64,000 Question (1955-57)
Gunsmoke (1957-61)
Wagon Train (1961-62)
The Beverly Hillbillies (1962-64)
Bonanza (1964-67)
The Andy Griffith Show (1967-68)
Rowan and Martin's Laugh-In (1968-70)
Marcus Welby, M.D. (1970-71)
All in the Family (1971-76)
Happy Days (1976-77)
Laverne and Shirley (1977-78)
Three's Company (1978-79)
60 Minutes (1979-80, 1982-83)
Dallas (1980-82; 1983-85)

Some Top Favorites & Cult Classics

ALFRED HITCHCOCK PRESENTS (1955-65)

Though Alfred Hitchcock had made some 40 films by 1955, for millions his stint as host of this popular anthology series was what made him a legend.

Hitchcock opened every episode with a droll greeting of "Good evening," followed by an opening commentary that ostensibly set the stage for that night's drama but was, in fact, just an excuse for some macabre humor.

Best of all, Hitchcock reserved his best deadpan disdain for the commercials that followed his comments. With these comments, he won the hearts of viewers who, of course, could not have agreed more.

Ironically, the sponsors ended up looking good because they were perceived as good sports for letting Hitchcock get his digs in at their commercials.

Most of the stories in *Alfred Hitchcock Presents* were "tales with a twist." At the end of many of them, the "bad guys" apparently got off free. As a result, Hitchcock's wrap-up comments frequently included the assurance that lawful authorities (or something even worse) eventually caught up with the guilty parties. This apparently made the network censors feel more comfortable with the dramas.

In 1985, NBC brought back the *Alfred Hitchcock Presents* anthology, using a new process to add color to Hitchcock's old black-and-white comment segments. The stories themselves were newly filmed.

THE AVENGERS (1966-69)

Though *The Avengers* had been on British TV since 1961, it did not reach the U.S. audiences until March 1966, when ABC bought it as a mid-season replacement.

ABC aired more than 70 episodes of *The Avengers* episodes on and off until 1969. Yet during that time, American audiences saw only two of Patrick Macnee's four partners: Diana Rigg as Emma Peel and Linda Thorson as Tara King.

The original partner of Jonathan Steed (Macnee's character) had been a man—Dr. David Keel (Ian Hendry). The series' title came from this initial teaming: Keel's wife had been murdered, so Keel and his mysterious friend Steed teamed up to find the killer and avenge the death.

Macnee's second partner was Honor Blackman as Cathy Gale, an independent, self-sufficient woman. She left the series to star in the 1964 James Bond film *Goldfinger.*

Diana Rigg's character, Emma Peel, followed in the footsteps of Gale, working with Steed as a strong but sexy partner who could

The Avengers

take care of herself. The team of Rigg and Macnee was the one that made the series a hit with American audiences.

DALLAS (1978-)

Dallas made headlines worldwide in 1980 with its most famous season-ending cliff-hanger: Who shot J.R.?

The question became the subject of intense speculation. In Great Britain (where gambling on virtually anything is legal), odds were quoted at 20-1 that J.R. Ewing had shot himself.

On November 21, 1980, CBS earned record-high ratings as millions tuned in to learn who *did* shoot J.R. So that no one would leak

Dallas

the answer, five different scenes were shot, each revealing a different character as the killer: Cliff Barnes (J.R.'s hated enemy), Jock Ewing (J.R.'s father), Ellie Ewing (J.R.'s mother), Sue Ellen Ewing (J.R.'s wife), and Kristin Shepherd (Sue Ellen's sister).

*P*erhaps with an eye on the British betting parlors, there was even a sequence filmed in which J.R. shot himself. In the scene, Larry Hagman (who played J.R. Ewing) pulled the trigger, then gave a perfect "how-in-the-world-did-I-do-THAT?" expression.

*W*hen the episode finally rolled, it revealed that Kristin, J.R.'s former mistress and Sue Ellen's sister, had pulled the trigger.

DOCTOR WHO (1963-   )

Doctor Who comes from the planet Gallifrey. As one of the race of Time Lords on the planet, he knows the secrets of time and space travel and uses a vehicle known as the *TARDIS* to carry him throughout the universe.

TARDIS is an acronym for "Time and Relative Dimensions in Space."

The unlikely appearance of the *TARDIS*, which looks like a London police phone booth, came about like this: The chameleon circuit (which allows the *TARDIS* to assume any shape appropriate to its environment) broke while the vehicle was in the shape of a phone booth. Over several hundred years the Doctor has never gotten around to fixing it.

On the show, the character Doctor Who is over 750 years old.

Six actors have played Doctor Who: William Hartnell (the First Doctor); Patrick Troughton (the Second Doctor); Jon Pertwee (the Third Doctor); Tom Baker (the Fourth Doctor); Peter Davison (the Fifth Doctor); and Colin Baker (the Sixth Doctor)—Colin and Tom Baker are not related.

How come six actors who look so different could all play the same role in *Doctor Who?* Each of the performers is presented as a new "regeneration" of the Doctor. So viewers are meeting the same person but in a different body.

Doctor Who can regenerate twelve times. He's currently on his fifth regeneration.

The six "segments" to the Key of Time were all disguised, but can you name the disguises? They were: a rock made of the mineral Jethrik; the planet Calufrax; a pendant made of the Great Seal of the planet Diplos; a statue; a relic swallowed by a giant squid-like creature; and the Princess Astra of Atrios (Lalla Ward).

Remember K-9, the dog-like mobile computer in *Doctor Who*? K-9 was introduced in the story "The Invisible Enemy" when he left his creator, Dr. Marius, to travel with the Doctor. Later, the Doctor built two other K-9 models.

U.N.I.T. was an international military force set up to deal with extraterrestrial threats to Earth. The name was an acronym for United Nations Intelligence Task Force.

Doctor Who is not actually the Doctor's name. He is known simply as the Doctor. *Doctor Who* is just the title of the series—and the question posed by some people upon first meeting him: "Doctor . . . ? Doctor Who?"

THE GREATEST AMERICAN HERO (1981-83)

William Katt (son of *Perry Mason*'s Barbara Hale and *Kit Carson*'s Bill Williams) played the part of high-school teacher Ralph Hinkley, who became a superhero when he received a red "supersuit" from a visiting alien spaceship.

Ralph worked with FBI agent Bill Maxwell (Robert Culp) who was also there when "the little green guys" (as he called them) left Ralph the suit. Unfortunately for both of them, Ralph promptly lost the instructions that came with it.

Unlike Superman's Lois Lane, Ralph Hinkley's girl friend, Pam Davidson (played by Connie Sellecca) learned her boyfriend's secret almost immediately, and soon became an essential part of the team.

Shortly after *The Greatest American Hero* went on the air, John Hinckley attempted to assassinate U.S. President Ronald Reagan. For a short while after that, Ralph Hinkley was referred to simply as "Mr. H," and the name "Hanley" was dubbed over existing episodes.

LOU GRANT (1977-82)

When *The Mary Tyler Moore Show* ended its run in the spring of 1977, the MTM production company took the unusual step of spinning off the popular character of Lou Grant into an hour-long drama, rather than into another half-hour sitcom series. The strategy worked, and the program played for five seasons.

Ed Asner continued in the role of Lou Grant as the character moved from Minneapolis-St. Paul to Los Angeles, changing jobs from television news producer to city editor of the Los Angeles *Tribune*.

The two top reporters under Lou's command included Joe Rossi (Robert Walden) and Billie Newman (Linda Kelsey). Dennis "Animal" Price (Daryl Anderson) was one of the paper's photographers and Art Donovan (Jack Bannon) was Lou's assistant.

Mason Adams played Lou's immediate superior, Charlie Hume. Ironically, Adams was probably most familiar to viewers through his voice. He had long been a widely used announcer for various commercial products on both television and radio.

Nancy Marchand played Margaret Pynchon, the owner of the newspaper. Back in the "Golden Age of Television" during the 1950s, Marchand appeared in the teleplay *Marty*, playing opposite Rod Steiger as the girl Marty meets at a dance.

THE MAN FROM U.N.C.L.E. (1964-68)

Originally titled *Solo* but changed to *The Man From U.N.C.L.E.* before its debut in the fall of 1964, this was television's answer to the increasingly popular series of James Bond theatrical films.

There was even a vague tie-in with Ian Fleming, creator of James Bond. The name of the lead character, Napoleon Solo (played by Robert Vaughn) had been used by Fleming himself in one of his novels. He gave the *U.N.C.L.E.* producers permission to use it for the series.

Solo did not work *solo*. He was teamed with Illya Kuryakin (David McCallum), and together the two men from U.N.C.L.E. set off to thwart international villains, who were frequently in the employ of the arch-enemy organization, THRUSH.

According to the television series, THRUSH was not an abbreviation for anything. However, in the series of tie-in paperback U.N.C.L.E. novels, it was suggested that THRUSH really stood for the Technological Hierarchy for the Removal of Undesirables and the Subjugation of Human-

The Man From U.N.C.L.E.

ity. There was no disagreement about the meaning of U.N.C.L.E.—it stood for the United Network Command for Law and Enforcement.

Leo G. Carroll played the head of U.N.C.L.E., Alexander Waverly, who spoke with his agents through a world-wide communications system via a special pen they carried.

In April 1983, CBS reunited Solo and Kuryakin in a special made-for-TV movie entitled "The Fifteen Years Later Affair."

MAVERICK (1957-62)

At the time when westerns were saturating the television airwaves, *Maverick* was in a class by itself. The program was done with a wry sense

Maverick

of humor, emphasizing the fact that the Maverick brothers (James Garner as Bret and Jack Kelly as Bart) preferred gambling over such traditional western-hero activities as gunfights and horse chases.

After three seasons, James Garner and Warner Bros. became locked in a dispute, so Garner left the series. He was replaced by Roger Moore as cousin Beau Maverick, but that lasted less than a season. The studio then introduced another "brother," Brent (Robert Colbert), but he lasted only a few episodes.

For its final season, *Maverick* mixed new episodes starring Jack Kelly with old episodes starring James Garner.

Maverick was created by Roy Huggins, who later worked with James Garner on *The Rockford Files* (1974-80).

MURDER, SHE WROTE (1984-)

After nearly 40 years of successful theatrical films and stage work, Angela Lansbury came to television to play a mystery writer and amateur sleuth, Jessica Fletcher.

Lansbury was perfect for the role. In fact, she had already played a kindred character, Agatha Christie's spinster supersleuth Miss Marple, in the 1983 theatrical film *The Mirror Crack'd.*

Richard Levinson and William Link, who had created *Columbo*, helped co-create *Murder, She Wrote*, bringing to the series their longstanding affection for genuine mysteries with real clues that the audience can follow.

As Mrs. Fletcher solved each case, she advanced her writing career as well—inevitably the stories became the basis for yet another of her mysteries.

THE PAPER CHASE (1978-79; 1983-)

Based on a successful feature film starring John Houseman, *The Paper Chase* presented the trials and tribulations of first-year law students at a prestigious Eastern university. Houseman repeated his role as the imposing Professor Charles Kingsfield, who taught freshmen Contract Law.

The rest of the cast was entirely new for the television series, including James Stephens as James T. Hart, an eager new student from the Midwest who was determined to learn all he could from Kingsfield.

The program won high praise from critics, but never attracted big ratings. CBS dropped it after just one season. Unlike most other prestige programs, *The Paper Chase* took on a new life after the cancellation.

First, selected episodes of the series were rerun on public television stations. Then, 20th Century-Fox began production of all new episodes as *The Paper Chase* became the first network series to continue with new episodes on cable. In 1983, the Showtime cable network began airing *The Paper Chase: The Second Year.*

60 MINUTES (1968-)

For years, the television networks regarded news documentaries and specials as money-losing, prestige ventures because they never attracted high ratings. At first, *60 Minutes* seemed to be more of the same.

In the mid-1970s, *60 Minutes* began to change all that. First, it cracked the top 20. Then, the top ten. In the 1979 season, *60 Minutes* achieved the ultimate television honor: It was the number-one series for the entire season. Since then, the show has been a consistent top ten hit.

The hosts/correspondents for *60 Minutes* have included Mike Wallace, Harry Reasoner, Morley Safer, Dan Rather, Ed Bradley, and Diane Sawyer.

STAR TREK (1966-69)

The starship *Enterprise* was described in the opening credits as being on a "five-year mis-

Star Trek

sion." In 1969, when NBC canceled the show, it seemed that the prediction had been overly optimistic.

*T*wo decades later, that five-year estimate seems conservative. *Star Trek* has become one of the most popular syndicated series in television history. It has spawned three theatrical feature films; and both the films and the original TV episodes are big sellers in the videotape and videodisc market.

Sitcoms of the Seventies & Eighties

ALL IN THE FAMILY (1971-83)

All in the Family was based on a successful British sitcom, *'Till Death Do Us Part*, in which a bigoted father was constantly at odds with his live-in son-in-law.

In the British program the conflicts represented a clash of classes. However, *All in the Family* made its mark by dealing with hot, topical issues in the format of a television sitcom.

All in the Family was not immediately embraced when first proposed by Norman Lear and Bud Yorkin. It had been around CBS and ABC in pilot form since early 1968. It was not until January 1971 that the program premiered on CBS.

Over the next decade, *All in the Family* became an American institution, as viewers watched Archie and Edith Bunker, and Gloria and Mike Stivic, grow together. Eventually, Archie Bunker's favorite chair ended up on display in the Smithsonian Institute in Washington D.C.

THE BOB NEWHART SHOW (1972-78)

In this series, Bob Newhart played Robert Hartley, a successful Chicago psychologist. Suzanne Pleshette played his wife, Emily.

Bill Daily played their next-door neighbor, Howard Borden, an airline navigator who operated on his own plane of reality. He inevitably popped by the Hartley apartment just in time for dinner, generally misunderstanding whatever was going on.

Though filmed in Los Angeles, the series did frequently display its Chicago roots. The opening and closing credits were shot along Chicago's lakefront, and Dr. Hartley's office was in an easily identifiable bank building (Uptown Federal Savings) on Michigan Avenue.

Like Newhart, who had grown up in Chicago, Dr. Hartley had attended Loyola University, a private college on the city's north side. He was also a big sports fan, and was always cheering for the Bears football team or Loyola's basketball team.

Dr. Hartley usually conducted group sessions, allowing a great deal of interaction with such patients as paranoid Elliott Carlin (Jack Riley), eternally henpecked Emile Peterson (John Fiedler), and perpetually knitting Mrs. Bakerman (Florida Friebus).

For the final season of the program, Newhart cut back his appearances a bit. For some episodes Bob Hartley was "on the road" promoting a popular psychology book he had written. Most of his bits were done with him standing at a pay telephone in an airport, usually talking to Emily.

In the last episode of the series, Bob decided on a career change and accepted a teaching position out West. Like the final episode of *The Mary Tyler Moore Show*, the cast had a tearful goodbye scene, then went out singing. Their wrap-up song: "Oklahoma!"

BOSOM BUDDIES (1980-82)

Bosom Buddies borrowed the main gag from the 1959 film *Some Like It Hot* (two men in drag) and used it effectively as the basis for a weekly sitcom.

Tom Hanks and Peter Scolari played Kip Wilson and Henry Desmond, two young men working for a New York advertising agency. Soon after their supercheap apartment was demolished, they discovered that there was another supercheap place available—the classy Susan B. Anthony hotel, which was open only to women. Desperate, they disguised themselves as two women: Buffy and Hildegard, Kip and Henry's sisters.

The dressed-in-drag idea was pushed to the background during the second season, as they revealed their dual identities to a few of the women at the hotel and concentrated instead on setting up their own production agency (60 Seconds Street).

Bosom Buddies was never a big hit, but the program was widely admired, especially for the strong characterizations by Hanks and Scolari. Soon after the program was canceled, Scolari joined the cast of *Newhart*, while Hanks began to build a career in feature films *(Splash, Bachelor Party,* and *Volunteers).*

CHEERS (1982-)

Created by the producers of *Taxi*, this ensemble sitcom set in a Boston bar (called "Cheers") experienced changes in its premise in each of its first three seasons. Each one involved the central characters of Sam Malone (Ted Danson), owner of the bar, and Diane Chambers (Shelley Long), an overeducated intellectual who worked as a barmaid.

In the first season, Sam and Diane constantly traded barbs, claiming to hate each other. At the close of the season, though, a passionate argument led to the beginning of a passionate affair.

At the end of the second season, Sam and Diane had a bitter break-up. For the third, Diane was back at the bar with a new boyfriend (her former therapist), once again pretending not to care about Sam.

A real-life double pregnancy caused some complications in the third season, when both Shelley Long and Rhea Perlman (who played Carla, another waitress at the bar) told the producers they were expecting.

The producers decided to let Perlman's character, Carla, become pregnant as well, so as her pregnancy progressed, the cameras and scripts played up the situation.

The opposite approach was taken with Long's character of Diane. She was hidden behind the bar, filmed from the back, and eventually packed off to Europe, where she was dressed in bulky clothes while in places such as Switzerland. Apparently, with Diane trying to decide between Sam and her current boyfriend, a pregnancy would have only complicated matters. For instance, who would have been the father?

One unfortunate change necessary for the fourth season was the replacement of the character Ernie "Coach" Pantusso (Nicholas Colasanto), Sam's former baseball coach and chief bartender. Colasanto died toward the end of filming the third season's episodes.

THE COSBY SHOW (1984-)

Bill Cosby brought a lifetime of observations about growing up and raising a family to this NBC sitcom, which quickly became the hottest show on television. It was like seeing all of the comedian's greatest personal routines brought to life.

In the pilot episode of the series, Cosby's TV family included four children: daughters Denise (Lisa Bonet), Vanessa (Tempestt Bledsoe), and Rudy (Keshia Knight Pulliam), and son Theodore (Malcolm-Jamal Warner). As the series went on, a fourth (eldest) daughter turned up, Sondra (Sabrina LeBeauf), who was away at college.

Bill Cosby's real-life family also consists of four daughters (Erika, Erinn, Ense, and Evin) and a son.

Phylicia Ayers-Allen played Clair Huxtable, a successful lawyer. Bill Cosby played her husband, Cliff, a successful doctor.

DIFF'RENT STROKES (1978-)

Conrad Bain played Philip Drummond, a white millionaire businessman and widower who lived on Park Avenue with his daughter Kimberly (Dana Plato) and his two adopted sons, Willis (Todd Bridges) and Arnold (Gary Coleman), who were both black.

Willis and Arnold had been the sons of Drummond's former housekeeper, who had asked him before she died to take care of them. He kept his promise.

Eventually, Drummond expanded his household even further when he married Maggie McKinney (played by Dixie Carter), who brought her own young son, Sam (Danny Cooksey), into the family.

In one episode of *Diff'rent Strokes*, First Lady Nancy Reagan made a special guest appearance in a story dealing with fighting drug abuse.

FAMILY TIES (1982-)

What happens when former college radicals grow up? They become middle-aged parents with children who just don't understand them! The generation gap is back to haunt them.

Meredith Baxter Birney and Michael Gross played Elyse and Steve Keaton, an architect and manager of a local public TV station. Their children included Jennifer (Tina Yothers), Mallory (Justine Bateman), and Alex (Michael J. Fox). Appropriately, Alex was a *Wall Street Journal* type who found his parents' wide-eyed liberalism virtually impossible to fathom.

Family Ties was a moderately successful program until the fall of 1984, when it was slotted after the new *Cosby* show. Then, it joined *Cosby* in flying through the Nielsen ratings roof, as both built up an audience interested in watching family sitcoms.

Family Ties received a further boost going into the following season when Michael J. Fox starred in the successful summer film, *Back to the Future*.

HAPPY DAYS (1974-84)

Happy Days was created by veteran sitcom writer Garry Marshall, who had worked on *The Dick Van Dyke Show* and produced *The Odd Couple*.

Marshall's pilot for *Happy Days* first aired as an episode of the comedy anthology *Love, American Style*, and featured Ron Howard as Richie Cunningham, Marion Ross as his mother, Marion, and Harold Gould as his father, Howard. That story (called "Love and the Happy Day") was set in the 1950s, as the Cunningham family became one of the first on the block to own a television set.

At first, Marshall's pilot did not get anywhere, but when George Lucas scored a big theatrical hit with *American Graffiti*, using not only the same nostalgic setting but also including Ron Howard in the cast, ABC got interested.

There were a few changes, including the casting of Tom Bosley as Richie's father and the addition of a new character, Arthur "Fonzie" Fonzarelli, played by Henry Winkler.

Happy Days

Happy Days became the cornerstone for ABC's rise to the top of the ratings in the mid- to late 1970s. The program had a pair of direct prime time spin-offs, *Laverne & Shirley* and *Joanie Loves Chachi*, and also served as the basis for a Saturday morning cartoon show.

The pilot for *Mork & Mindy* also aired as an episode of *Happy Days*.

THE MARY TYLER MOORE SHOW (1970-77)

Mary Tyler Moore's breakthrough ensemble comedy launched one of the most prestigious production companies in television history, MTM. It was an auspicious beginning.

Moore herself had strong credentials as a comedienne with her character of Laura Petrie, from *The Dick Van Dyke Show*. She was sur-

The Mary Tyler Moore Show

rounded by a supporting cast so strong that each one went on to star in another successful television series.

Mary Tyler Moore played Mary Richards, a single woman of about 30 who comes to Minneapolis after calling it quits with her boyfriend. Originally, she was supposed to have left her hometown after a divorce, but that was considered too controversial for the time.

In Minneapolis, Mary worked for a low-rated television news department (WJM-TV) with an incompetent anchorman, Ted Baxter (played by Ted Knight).

Ironically, after seven seasons, the series ended with Ted Baxter being the only one retained when new management took over the station.

For the wrap-up episode, the entire cast joined together in a tearful farewell, ending with a rousing rendition of the song "It's a Long Way to Tipperary."

M.T.M. ALUMS

All of the main performers on *The Mary Tyler Moore Show* went on to star in other series:

Ed Asner in *Lou Grant*
Ted Knight in *Too Close for Comfort*
Gavin MacLeod in *The Love Boat*
Valerie Harper in *Rhoda*
Cloris Leachman in *Phyllis*
Betty White in *The Golden Girls*
Georgia Engel in *The Goodtime Girls*
Even Mary Tyler Moore came back in *Mary*

M*A*S*H (1972-83)

*M*A*S*H* barely made it through its first season, turning in dismal ratings in its Sunday night time slot surrounded by *Anna and the King* and *The Sandy Duncan Show.*

Despite its poor early showing, CBS executives felt that *M*A*S*H* had potential, and to help its ratings it was given a golden slot between two established Saturday night hits—*All in the Family* and *The Mary Tyler Moore Show.*

Even after *M*A*S*H* began rerun syndication on local stations, first-run episodes still continued to do well. One possible reason for this resilience was that *M*A*S*H* had undergone so many cast and writing changes that it seemed like a different show every few years.

M*A*S*H

*T*he most dramatic change in the *M*A*S*H* cast occurred after the program's third season, when both Wayne Rogers (Trapper John McIntire) and McLean Stevenson (Col. Henry Blake) left the cast. Their replacements were veteran television actor Harry Morgan as Col. Sherman Potter and Mike Farrell as Captain B.J. Hunnicutt.

*T*he final episode of *M*A*S*H* was a two-and-one-half hour special ("Goodbye, Farewell, and Amen") that became the highest rated program in television history.

MORK & MINDY (1978-82)

*T*he pilot for this series appeared as an episode of *Happy Days* in which Richie Cunningham met alien Mork (Robin Williams). Mork wanted to take Richie back to Ork, his home planet. Fonzie came to the rescue and as Mork and the Fonz faced off . . . Richie woke up.

Mork & Mindy

As a postscript to the story, Richie did a double take when a farmer came to the front door asking directions—because he looked just like Mork.

The idea of involving an alien in *Happy Days* came from producer Garry Marshall, who said that one of his children asked if there could be a space invader story on TV.

Each episode of *Mork & Mindy* ended with a report by Mork to his boss, Orson, on the planet Ork. Orson was clearly an allusion to Orson Welles (perpetrator of the "War of the Worlds" Halloween radio scare), with many of Mork's comments directed at Orson's girth.

In an effort to boost sagging ratings in the fourth season, Jonathan Winters joined the cast as the newly hatched child of Mork and Mindy. That failed to work, and the show ended in the fall of 1982. The characters continued for another year as a Saturday morning cartoon show.

The Odd Couple

THE ODD COUPLE (1970-75)

Tony Randall and Jack Klugman played Felix Unger (the neat one) and Oscar Madison (the messy one) in this successful adaptation of the hit play (and movie) by Neil Simon.

At the end of the five-year run of the series, Randall and Klugman toured briefly in a new theatrical production of the original Neil Simon play.

In 1982, the TV series was briefly and unsuccessfully revived as *The New Odd Couple*, with Ron Glass as Felix and Desmond Wilson as Oscar.

SOAP (1977-81)

This comic soap opera stirred quite a scandal even before its first episode aired. During production, word leaked out that one of the characters was going to seduce a Catholic priest in church. Religious groups throughout the country wrote letters and organized protests. Some Catholic newspapers ran a coupon on the front page for readers to clip and send to ABC.

In response, ABC arranged for the series to air at a later time in the central time zone and also promised to add a viewer discretion notice before each episode.

All of this turned out to be a bonanza of publicity for the program and virtually guaranteed top ten ratings. *Soap* premiered as one of the most successful shows of the new season. It also evolved into one of the funniest, with the controversial aspects overshadowed by the satiric situations and characters.

As it turned out, the priest was not seduced in church, though he did find himself in love with a beautiful woman. Eventually, he decided to leave the priesthood and marry her. They had a child—who was born possessed by the devil and had to be exorcised.

Veteran singer and stage performer Robert Guillaume played Benson, family butler to the Tate household. In 1979, his character was spun off into a separate show, where he eventually moved from household manager at the state's governor's mansion to lieutenant governor.

THREE'S COMPANY (1977-84)

The premise for this series was taken from a British program called *Man About the House,* in which a young man shared an apartment with two attractive women so that all of them could save on rent. Nothing sexual ever happened between them.

For American consumption, an extra twist was added to explain why the landlord would allow such an arrangement. He was told that Jack Tripper (the "man about the house" played by John Ritter) was gay.

At first, Jack's two roommates were Janet Wood (Joyce DeWitt) and Chrissy Snow (Suzanne Somers). In the fifth season, Somers was phased out of the show after producers balked at her salary demands. Instead, they virtually wrote Somers out of the program for the last year of her contract, relegating her to one brief scene each week talking to the rest of the cast by telephone.

As Suzanne Somers was slowly being phased out of *Three's Company,* Jenilee Harrison came aboard as Chrissy's cousin, Cindy Snow. Beginning in the fall of 1981, Somers' character was replaced by Terri Alden (Priscilla Barnes), a completely new roommate for Jack and Janet.

The other major cast change in *Three's Company* occurred in the fourth season when landlords Stanley and Helen Roper (Norman Fell and Audra Lindley) were spun off into their own series, *The Ropers.* Don Knotts took their place as landlord Ralph Furley.

WKRP IN CINCINNATI (1978-82)

*W**KRP in Cincinnati* was given both very good and very strange treatment by CBS. At first, the network gave the program a rare second chance when it failed to do well in its first few weeks. The show was pulled from its time slot and given several months to retool.

When it returned, *WKRP* was given the golden time slot after the top-rated *M*A*S*H.* But it soon became one of CBS's most-often shifted shows, changing time slots six times in the next 18 months.

Ironically, just after it was canceled, *WKRP* achieved some of its highest ratings ever. Since then, it has done quite well in syndicated reruns.

---

20 TV SHOWS WITH THEME SONGS YOU CAN PROBABLY HUM IN THE SHOWER

The Addams Family
Batman
The Beverly Hillbillies ("The Ballad of Jed Clampett")
Bonanza
Car 54, Where Are You?
Dragnet
The Dick Van Dyke Show
The Greatest American Hero ("Believe It Or Not")
Happy Days
The Honeymooners
I Love Lucy
*M*A*S*H*
The Mickey Mouse Club

Mission: Impossible
Mr. Ed
My Three Sons
Secret Agent
77 Sunset Strip
Welcome Back, Kotter
Zorro

Sitcoms Before the Seventies

THE ADVENTURES OF OZZIE AND HARRIET (1952-66)

America grew up with the Nelson family, from the early 1950s to the mid-1960s. During this time, everyone asked themselves at least once: What does Ozzie *do* for a living? Why is he *always* at home? When the program began on radio, there was no such confusion. Ozzie was a successful band leader, Harriet was his star vocalist, and the stories revolved around their adventures at home and at work. For television, viewers were simply never shown the family's source of income, only their life at home (modeled after the Nelson's real-life home in Hollywood).

The focus of attention in the series was on the Nelson children, David and Ricky, as they faced the normal problems of growing up: girls, dates, school, cars, and (of course) money. Beginning in 1957, the show developed a very special attraction: Rick (as he preferred to be called) had become a teenage singing star.

Rick Nelson's first hit was "I'm Walkin'," backed with "Teenager's Romance." Soon practically every episode featured a closing concert segment with Rick singing his latest release. Over the course of the series, he placed more than a dozen records in the top ten.

When Rick and David grew up, went to college, and got married in real life, the same thing happened on the show. Their wives were added to the cast, expanding the opening credits to include Ozzie, Harriet, David, June, Rick, and Kris.

BACHELOR FATHER (1957-62)

John Forsythe played Bentley Gregg, the "bachelor father" of the series. He was legal guardian to his niece, Kelly (Noreen Corcoran), whose parents had been killed in a car crash when she was 13.

Bentley was a successful Hollywood attorney who drove a stylish convertible and lived in a posh home in Beverly Hills. Peter Tong (played by Sammee Tong) was his indispensable housekeeper. The family's pet shaggy dog was named Jasper.

After *Bachelor Father*, John Forsythe appeared as the star of two other sitcoms (*The John Forsythe Show* and *To Rome With Love*) before shifting over to an adventure series (the voice of Charlie in *Charlie's Angels*), then a prime time soap opera (*Dynasty*).

THE BEVERLY HILLBILLIES (1962-71)

The premise was simple: Take a poor mountaineer (Buddy Ebsen as Jed Clampett) who could barely keep his family fed, and make him wealthy beyond belief. How? One day when he was shooting at some food, he hit the ground instead. And up came the bubbling crude. "Oil, that is. Black gold. Texas tea."

Jed's kinfolks said he should head west with his new-found wealth. "So they loaded up the truck and they moved to Beverly. Hills, that is."

Relocated in California, the Clampetts deposited their boodle in the Commerce Bank of Beverly Hills, thereby winning the slobbering affection of Milburn Drysdale (Raymond Bailey),

The Beverly Hillbillies

president of the institution. Miss Jane Hathaway (Nancy Kulp), his number one assistant, took personal care of the Clampetts, helping them adjust as best as they could to Beverly Hills society.

Despite Miss Hathaway's efforts, the Clampetts never really lost their Ozark ways. Granny (Irene Ryan) was always suspicious of newfangled city ways. Elly May (Donna Douglas) preferred to take care of her critters. And Jethro (Max Baer) was like a kid in a toy shop. He never tired of playing with "them swimmin' pools and movie stars."

"The Ballad of Jed Clampett" (the series theme song) was sung by Jerry Scoggins. Lester Flatt and Earl Scruggs wrote and played the theme.

THE BRADY BUNCH (1969-74)

To set up *The Brady Bunch*, a widower (Robert Reed as Mike Brady) with three boys married a widow (Florence Henderson as Carol Martin) with three girls. The result? The Brady Bunch.

The Brady girls were Marcia (Maureen McCormick), Jan (Eve Plumb), and Cindy (Susan Olsen), while the Brady boys were Greg (Barry Williams), Peter (Christopher Knight), and Bobby (Mike Lookinland).

Ann B. Davis rounded out the cast as Alice Nelson, the Brady's housekeeper. Back in the 1950s, she had played a "gal Friday" named Shultzy in a very different setting: the office of a swinging bachelor photographer in *The Bob Cummings Show*, also known as *Love That Bob*.

In addition to the half-hour sitcom, the Brady characters subsequently appeared in an animated cartoon version (*The Brady Kids*), an hour-long variety show (*Brady Bunch Hour*), and a mini-series (*The Brady Brides*).

THE DICK VAN DYKE SHOW (1961-66)

Carl Reiner originally created this series (then called *Head of the Family*) as a vehicle for himself. He cast himself as Rob Petrie, head writer for a comedy-variety series. Barbara Britton played his wife, Laura.

When that did not sell, Reiner revamped the cast, including a new lead, Dick Van Dyke. For this version, Reiner gave himself the role of Alan Brady, host of the comedy-variety program that Rob Petrie wrote for.

The Dick Van Dyke Show

Morey Amsterdam and Rose Marie played Rob's wisecracking fellow writers, Buddy Sorrell and Sally Rogers. Most of Buddy's in-house barbs were directed at the program's producer, Mel Cooley (Richard Deacon), brother-in-law of Alan Brady.

At home, Mary Tyler Moore played Laura Petrie. Ann Morgan Guilbert and Jerry Paris played next-door-neighbors Jerry and Millie Helper. Paris also directed many episodes of the show.

THE GEORGE BURNS AND GRACIE ALLEN SHOW (1950-58)

George Burns and Gracie Allen made a seemingly effortless transition from radio to television, turning deceptively simple misunderstandings into timeless comedy.

Gracie took care of the illogical logic, while George stood by as narrator and observer, commenting on the action—and getting in a few jokes on the side.

The program took on a touch of the surreal when George watched the action of that week's episode (while still in progress) on a television in his upstairs den. From there, he saw how the plot was going by looking at other characters, such as Blanche and Harry Morton, announcer Harry Von Zell, or son Ronnie Burns.

Once in a while, after Gracie had done some particularly absurd thing, George would turn to the camera and say, "Because I love her, that's why."

After the *Burns and Allen* show, George appeared without Gracie (who had retired from active performing) in three other series: *The George Burns Show*, *Wendy and Me*, and *The George Burns Comedy Week*.

GREEN ACRES (1965-71)

This was Paul Henning's flip side to his popular *Beverly Hillbillies* series. Instead of country folk moving to the city, two wealthy city dwellers moved to the country.

Eddie Albert played Oliver Douglas, a successful lawyer who had always dreamed of living on a farm, and Eva Gabor played Lisa Douglas, who dreamed of moving back to New York City.

Green Acres also tied in to another Henning series, *Petticoat Junction*, because the action was set in the same town—Hooterville. Some of the same characters (such as store owner Sam Drucker) were regulars on both shows, and others made occasional guest appearances.

Perhaps the most unusual character in Hooterville was Arnold the pig (full name: Arnold Ziffel). Over the years, he played checkers, watched television, and even auditioned for a role in Hollywood.

I LOVE LUCY (1951-57)

On January 19, 1953, Lucille Ball gave birth to a healthy baby boy named after his father, Desi Arnaz. Later that same day, millions watched as Lucy Ricardo gave birth to a healthy baby boy named after his father, Ricky Ricardo.

I Love Lucy

The double drama of a real-life and fictional pregnancy was a classic moment in television history (and a publicity agent's dream). It practically overshadowed the inauguration of Dwight Eisenhower as U.S. President the following day, and it helped boost *I Love Lucy* into a long stint as the number-one series on television.

THE LIFE OF RILEY (1949-50; 1953-58)

There were two TV versions of this sitcom, which was based on a successful radio series from the 1940s. The first starred Jackie Gleason as the dumb but lovable Chester A. Riley, riveter at an aircraft plant. That lasted less than five months.

William Bendix, who had played the character in the radio version, assumed the role with an all-new cast for the revamped 1953 version. That was a success and lasted into the late 1950s.

Riley's trademark phrase when confronted with the latest complications to his life was: "What a revoltin' development this is!"

THE MANY LOVES OF DOBIE GILLIS (1959-63)

Dwayne Hickman played the perpetually heartstruck Dobie Gillis ("that's 'Dobie' with a 'b'!") in this series created by and based on stories written by Max Shulman.

Over the course of the series, Dobie and his "good buddy" Maynard G. Krebbs (Bob Denver) searched for the meaning of it all through high school, the army, and college.

Actually, Dobie was convinced he knew exactly what it was all about—women. He constantly pursued knockouts such as Thalia Menninger (Tuesday Weld) while ignoring the affections of classmate Zelda Gilroy (Sheila James).

Maynard, for his part, knew exactly what life was *not* about—work. He jumped at the very mention of the word.

On the other hand, Dobie's father, Herbert T. Gillis, was a staunch advocate of hard work. He dreamed that one day his son would take over the family business and become owner and operator of Gillis Grocery.

Dobie frequently puzzled out each week's developments while standing in front of a replica of Auguste Rodin's statue of "The Thinker."